GLOBAL AMBITIONS AND LOCAL IDENTITIES

GLOBAL AMBITIONS

AND

LOCAL IDENTITIES

An Israeli-American High Tech Merger

Galit Ailon

Berghahn Books

New York • Oxford

First published in 2007 by

Berghahn Books

www.berghahnbooks.com

© 2007 Galit Ailon

Library of Congress Cataloging-in-Publication Data

Ailon, Galit.
   Global ambitions and local identities : an Israeli-American high tech merger / by
Galit Ailon.
      p. cm.
   Includes bibliographical references and index.
   ISBN 1-84545-194-5 (hardcover : alk. paper)
   1. High technology industries—Mergers—Israel—Case studies.
   2. High technology industries—Mergers—United States—Case studies.
   3. Consolidation and merger of corporations—Case studies.   I. Title.

HC415.25.Z9H532 2007
338.8'3095694--dc22   2006100543

British Library Cataloguing in Publication Data
A catalogue record for this book is available from the British Library.

Grateful acknowledgment is made for permission to reprint excerpt from the song
lyric "Only Wanna Be With You," words by Rucker/Felber/Bryan/Sonefeld. Published
by Monica's Reluctance to Lob/EMI April Music Inc. Reprinted by permission of
EMI Music Publishing (Israel) Limited.

Grateful acknowledgment is made for permission to reprint excerpt from a *Dilbert*
cartoon. Copyright © 2006 Scott Adams Inc./Dist. By UFS Inc. Reprinted by
permission of United Media, Inc./gms Global Media Services GmbH.

Printed in the United States on acid-free paper

Contents

PART I

The Merger at Work:
Enacting a Separate Organizational Identity in Everyday Life

PART II

The Merger and the Worker: Aligning Identities, Centering Selves

CHAPTER 6
Work Identities: Difference and Dilemma

CHAPTER 7
Conclusion: Merging Ourselves Apart

Acknowledgements

I owe many thanks. My first debt is to Gideon Kunda who has been an excellent teacher. His ability to find social drama anywhere he looks and to combine analytical precision with extraordinary sensitivity to the people he studies has been a continual source of inspiration to me. Offering incisive criticism along with encouragement, Gideon has advanced my thinking and provided a rich soil from which my own intellectual stance could grow.

There are others who offered important contributions. David De Vries and Yinon Cohen each opened a critical door of opportunity for me and made perceptive comments. Eyal Ben-Ari, Guy Mundlak, Tal Simons, Nitza Yanay, and Jacqueline Waldren read drafts and contributed valuable insights and interpretations. Ely Weitz provided good advice, important remarks, and a lot of moral support. My fellow students, Karin Amit, Hadas Mandel, Ronit Nadiv, Yael Parag, and Sigal Shelach offered not only helpful suggestions but also a comforting sense of solidarity with regard to the hardships of graduate studies. Daniella Arieli has been invaluable as both a close friend and colleague. And Eyal Souday, my partner during the years of study, offered encouragement and unfailing support. I thank them all.

Some of my greatest debts, however, are to people whose names I cannot state. These are the people who allowed me to observe their work-lives, who shared their thoughts and let me into their world. In order to guard their anonymity, I cannot identify them here, but I feel I must express my gratitude to them. Without their generosity and cooperation this book would not have been possible.

I also thank the Department of Labor Studies at Tel Aviv University. Offering a highly professional doctoral program but at the same time posing reasonable temporal demands and providing employment, the department gives its graduate students—most of them, until now, women—the rare and truly equal opportunity to advance themselves without having to jeopardize their roles as parents and supporters of families. I am lucky to have been a part of this program and I am grateful for it. In addition, I am grateful to the Volovelsky-Karney Family Doctoral Fellowship, the Israel Foundation Trustees, and the Horowitz Institute for the scholarships that helped support my study in the program and my research activities.

Lastly, I thank the members of my family. My parents, Michal and Amit, offered reassurance and loving advice. Throughout, they were always ready and willing to lend me a helping hand with my own children. Without their assistance I do not know how I would have managed my multiple commitments. My sister Shiri, in her wise and straightforward way, has helped me out of a difficult period when writing (and other things) seemed stuck; my brother Nir, a technological genius, rescued me from a few potentially devastating computer disasters; and both were always there to offer a timely word of encouragement. As for my children, Ronnie and Ittay, from the moments they arrived—both, by the way, in the midst of this voyage—they have influenced my perspective and feeling about life in deeper ways than I can put in words. This book is dedicated to them.

CHAPTER 1

Introduction

"Here Comes the Groom"

January 14th, 1998 was a historic day for Isrocom.[1] It was the first day of a merger between this successful Israeli high-tech company and Amerotech, a New York based competitor. The special event was celebrated in the dining room with a festive breakfast buffet, rich and impressively decorated, complete with uniformed waiters and a busy social mingling commotion. In the corner of the dining room a video clip was played again and again on a large screen to the sound of two romantic pop songs: the English "Only Wanna be with You" and the Hebrew "Holding On." Flashy video scenes, alternating between New York and Tel Aviv, displayed happy workers waving "Hi"s and smiling "Welcome"s, and serious managers promising to "lead the whole world" in the companies' product field, assuring that "it is a great opportunity for the workers." At the entrance, two elegantly dressed women from the Human Resources Department greeted incoming members with an amused "Mazel Tov"[2] and offered them each a shiny pen resting in a box of black velvet, inscribed with the merged company's new name, "Globalint." When Nati, one of the senior managers responsible for the merger walked in, one of the women cried, "Here comes the groom! Happy merger, happy merger everyone!"

Judging by the looks of it, a happy merger it was. In the context of this pseudo-wedding celebration, the economic promises of globalization seemed as much within reach as a pile of soon-to-be-opened gifts. Though the success-statistics relating to the many companies that have taken this route before were not always encouraging,[3] nothing but optimism was reflected from the video clipped, corporate 'vow' exchange, the elegantly dressed hostesses, the food decor, the sweet pop songs, and the shiny pens in boxes of black velvet. Globalism appeared bright and full of prospects on that first merger day, and the company seemed to have made a full commitment to it.

Yet even on that festive merger-day event, some less romantic attitudes were being expressed by more spontaneous voices around the tables. Near my seat, for example, an engineer made a small parody of the American handshake by fiercely pumping his friend's hand, saying in English with an exaggerated accent, "Very nice to meet you." Grinning, his friend said, "Can you believe it? They only work until 4 p.m. over there." Engaging in a conversation about a recent visit of merger partners to the Operations Department, a member at the table described his guests as, "The typical American schmucks, babbling TQM all the time." A manager replied: "I'm not worried. They are the ones who should be worried. Most of the senior management team are our guys." When I asked another member who sat next to me what she thought about all this, she laughed, and, with a cynical imitation of the American accent, replied, "Oh . . . it is a great opportunity!" The event of a corporate "wedding" was thus re-created by participants at the table: while video-screened images were being displayed in romantic scenes of unity, members cynically distanced themselves from the bride-to-be. Sustaining a sense of a local[4] collective, they infused the global merger celebration with resistant national overtones. Members, in other words, were engaged in an identity project of their own, one quite distinct from the formal project that was repeatedly announced at the entrance with excited cries of "Mazel Tov."

To a large extent, the "wedding" between Isrocom and Amerotech is a part of a worldwide trend. As "Global Capitalism" takes root, marking a growing shift from a world economy consisting of reasonably distinct national units toward a more unified system with increasingly interrelated economic processes,[5] international mergers, acquisitions, joint ventures, and other forms of corporate globalization are becoming increasingly common. Many companies take advantage of falling trade barriers and the decreasing influence of national institutions of control over work and seek business opportunities throughout the world. Relying upon information technology, companies merge or emerge into global structures, overcoming geographical distance with a "space of flows" (Castells 1989) that collapses boundaries and converges places and time zones.

While apparent in all industries and work settings, these changes seem especially acute in the high-tech sector. Facing competition that is continually bolstered by rapid technological advance, high-tech companies typically adopt a global perspective. They search anywhere in the world for places that offer good access to telecommunications networks and air transportation as a means for maintaining close contact with clients. In addition, since they also seek to improve the knowledge pools that are their most crucial factor of production, high-tech companies locate their units in accordance with the availability of skilled manpower, often spatially differentiating production functions across the globe.[6] Moreover, alongside the global economic imperatives that relate to clients and labor, these companies are also pioneers in putting their own products and technological breakthroughs to use, as a means for integrating spatially dispersed units (Castells 1989: 74), customizing products, and enhancing productivity. To a large extent, then, high-tech companies are at the forefront of globalization, spearheading and setting in motion many of its business, trade, and technology processes.

As Globalint's first merger day celebration illustrates, the boundary-blurring processes of globalization raise issues of identity. While the concept "identity" perhaps connotes a sense of essential sameness—of an underlying, authentic, and persistent set of characteristics that is inherent in a person[7] and shared by a group—it is, as many contemporary writers maintain, largely premised upon the experience of difference. Adopting a constructivist outlook, theorists of identity increasingly argue that difference constitutes both the *impetus* and *means* for identity formations (for example, Hall, 1996b; Sarup, 1996): it is the underlying drive and overarching vocabulary through which notions of sameness are defined and come to be experienced as "real." Since globalization blurs or creates disjunctures in the traditional spatial, national, and cultural boundaries, saturating contemporary life with experiences of difference—of others and otherness—the impetus is accentuated and the means multiply. The questions "who am I?" or "who are we?" increasingly rise to the surface, and identities are re-examined and self-concepts redefined (Gupta & Ferguson, 1992).[8] New images of sameness are socially constructed through the working of different differences.

Based upon a year-long ethnographic study, this book sets out to examine such identity constructions within Isrocom.[9] Its goals are twofold. First, it seeks to scrutinize the resistant, local-organizational identity project that began around the tables on the first merger-day celebration. It asks what notions of organizational distinctiveness, what images of sameness, were enacted by Isrocom's members in everyday merger life? Second, it seeks to examine the project's interrelations with other salient identities that surfaced in the field: national identities, occupational identities, and hierarchical identities. The next two subsections will elaborate on these two goals.

The Organizational Identity as a Social Construct

Many researchers treat the organizational identity as a cognitive belief system. They see it as a neutral albeit managerially defined notion of what is central, distinctive, and enduring about the organization (Albert &

Whetten 1985) that is collectively internalized and utilized by members to define themselves (for example, Dutton, Dukerich & Harquail 1994; Elsbach & Kramer 1996; Reger, Gustafson, Demarie & Mullane 1994).[10] This concept is the organizational equivalent of the essentialist notion of identity as consisting of an inherent, persistent, underlying sameness (Czarniawska 1997), but, to a large extent, only as far as workers are concerned. Namely, while researchers in the field typically deny workers any active formative role, construing them as mere carriers of a common belief system about the organization, they do not deny but rather assume management's active role in defining this belief system. Granting the formal version of the organizational identity the status of an objective essence, these researchers treat workers as its passive carriers and managers as its active designers.

It seems, however, that workers too are constructors who are not passive in relation to managerially sanctioned versions of the organizational identity. Far from being total, management's control always leaves room for the development of resistant subjectivities and oppositional cultures. These play themselves out through the most minute and mundane aspects of everyday life (Jermier, Knights & Nord 1994), but seem to become especially evident at times of change (see Van Maanen 1998). Studies show, for example, that during dramatic shifts in organizational lives, members collectively sustain their own versions of and orientation toward the organization's history and achievements (Clark 1972), ideology and essence (Biggart 1977), and symbols (Pratt & Rafaeli 1997), bringing to light the cultural space that exists for defining the organizational identity outside or beyond whatever management formally decides it to be.

Indeed, this notion of cultural space seems true of any organization and especially of global ones. If, for example, in a non-global, American high-tech organization characterized by management's deliberate attempt to "engineer culture" there nonetheless remains space for an "active and artful construction" of the organizational self (Kunda 1992: 216), and in a small Japanese confectionary factory deploying the culturally compelling "company as family" idiom there remains space for the "multiplicities, open-endedness, and contradictions that inevitably accompany the crafting of identities" (Kondo 1990: 202–203),[11] then in global corporations this space seems especially spacious. Here, it has been shown, signs are recontextualized, cultural elements recombined, and meanings re-created (Van Maanen 1992). The formal, global version of membership is continually contested and dynamically negotiated (see Ó Riain 2000), becomes an object of members' resentment and resistance (Graham 1995), and, moreover, remains fraught with cultural crises and struggles even at the level of management (Hamada 1991). In global corporations, it seems, the means available for contesting the formal version of the organizational identity are abundant as is the cultural space within which it can occur.

The notion that identity is actively constructed rather than passively internalized resonates with a long tradition of sociological thought. The treatment of identity as a social construct dates back to the work of the "Early Interactionists"[12] who spoke of identity as a collectively defined, non-static, and symbolic process. Cooley (1902), perhaps the first leading contributor to this school of thought, focused on the primary group and argued that a child's identity is constructed through the imaginative sharing of meanings and judgment about his or her "looking glass self" with this group's others. Further elaborating this notion of construction, Thomas (1937) claimed that identities can be redefined throughout adulthood, flexibly springing from divergently constructed "definitions of the situation" that are taken on by individuals and their others. Similarly, Mead (1934) argued that people develop understandings about themselves in relation to meanings that are constructed through the symbolic process of "taking on the role of the other." Furthermore, in Mead's view people take quite an active role in these constructions, having a fairly large measure of ability to mold and remold, select and transform them in their internal dialogue between the "I" and the "me." Thus, according to the Early Interactionists, the meanings that arise in relation to group attachments are dynamic products of communication and interpretation processes that transpire between and, as Mead pointed out, within people.

Many of these insights have been taken up and further explored by later generations of researchers.[13] One of them, Erving Goffman (1959), focused less on the origin, development, and change of identities and more on their multiplicity. Developing a dramaturgical approach for the study of social interactions, he argued that identities are constructed for the purpose of managing impressions during everyday life performances, their shape changing in accordance with whatever it is that people seek to convince the others with whom they interact that they have become (see Van Maanen 1979). To use a term later developed by Stone (1962), identities are in this sense "situated," flexibly cast as social objects of divergent and shifting shapes in accordance with the interpretational mood of the interaction. While later writings, including those of Goffman himself, insisted that despite multiplicity some interrelations between identities remain,[14] the notion of multiplicity further highlights the ability that people have to manipulate symbols, words, and meanings and mold their identities in a flexible manner.[15]

This view has been taken to an extreme by postmodernist thinkers. Observing processes in the world today, postmodernists argue for the intensification of complexity: not only do people possess multiple identities but the symbolic means for constructing these identities are also multiplying, becoming increasingly fragmented as globalization progresses. Accordingly, there is today a postmodernist view of globalization as a kind of variegated, multicolored culture that consists of disjunctured flows, multiple and mobile meanings, creative juxtapositions, fusions, movements, and hybridizations (for example, Featherstone 1990; 1995; Appadurai 1990). As this view dissolves the once taken-for-granted linkage between cultures and bounded terrains (see, for example, Lavie & Swedenburg 1996), it challenges past notions of identities as fixed, stable, unitary, and homogeneous (Hall 1996b). In their place, it promotes a notion of self as decentered (Kondo 1990), consisting of identities that are multiple and mobile constructs; boundless interplays of differences; infinite combinations of cultural possibilities that can be picked up and chosen like clothes from shelves (see Mathews 2000). The reality of global cultural fragmentation in the postmodernist view thus accentuates the lack (or at least scarcity) of externally imposed identity essences, emphasizing instead the space, freedom, and possibilities that people have in defining their belongings.[16]

Thus, the tendency of many of the existing studies of organizational identity to overlook the issue of social construction does not coincide with a long tradition of thought. In her *Narrating the Organization,* Barbara Czarniawska (1997) seems to be the first to fully recognize this, claiming that the fact that "identity is created in the interactions between individuals in the social context" (p. 44) must be taken into account. Treating the organization as a superperson of sorts, she views the process of social construction as a storytelling institution, arguing that the organizational identity is a narrated autobiography that is created through conversations against a repertoire of accessible and flexible plots (the romantic marriage plot that was so visible on the first merger day seems a good example). Nevertheless, although no doubt a significant contribution, this conceptualization places a greater emphasis on the ways that members narrate sameness-over-time rather than on the way that they act upon and enact difference in everyday life. As this study examines a new merger, a context in which intergroup relations are something to be daily handled, it must focus not only on the means for constructing sameness, but also on the means for constructing difference: a handshake parody, a cynical imitation, remarks about how "they" work or why "they" should worry, and so forth.

In other words, following Czarniawska's lead, but not her path, this study explores how Isrocom's members socially constructed their organizational identity in daily merger life. In the spirit of studies of organizational change and globalization, it searches for the symbolic meanings that members actively attributed to this identity, the ways that they reacted to and resisted the global "married" version of it, and the social processes through which they designated a sense of collective distinctiveness. Its search, nevertheless, does not end here. As claimed, it has another, second goal.

Multiplicity and Interconnectedness

The organizational identity is not a universe unto itself. If only for the need to maintain an "illusion" of an integrated self—to mesh multiplicity within synchronous self-images[17]—it has a bearing upon other identities. This interconnectedness has been documented in several ethnographic studies of organizations. To take an extreme example, in *Asylums*, Goffman (1961) shows that the meanings that are generated by and that define membership in an organization lead to progressive changes in the broad system of beliefs a person has concerning who she is. Such effects are not confined to "total institutions." As Arlie Hochschild (1983) shows in *The Managed Heart* and Dorinne Kondo (1990) in *Crafting Selves*, conceptions of organizational membership and belonging have complex consequences in work organizations as well, influencing members' attitudes toward and perceptions of their other, non-organizational identities in ways that give rise to ironies and tensions.[18] Accordingly, in an attempt to offer a comprehensive account of the issue of identity, the second objective of this study is to examine the relationship between the processes of organizational identity construction that unfolded in the context of Isrocom's merger and other identities that came to the social fore.

This question of the relationship between the organizational and other identities is, it should be noted, of growing concern, especially with regard to global organizations. Most evident is the rising interest of managerially oriented writers in the relationship between the organizational and national identity. Namely, writers ask whether the formal, global identity of a transnational organization is or ever could be successful in overcoming members' existing national attachments. Their answers diverge. On one hand, writers such as Kenichi Ohmae, author of *The Borderless World* (1999) and *The End of the Nation State* (1995), claim that organizational globalization is indeed leading to the withering away of national attachments. Promoting a set of managerial techniques designed to homogenize the internal work-life of such organizations, Ohmae claims that within corporations reaching the highest stage of globalism "people may work 'in' different national environments, but are not 'of' them. What they are 'of' is the global corporation" (1999: 103). This view is supported by anthropologist Ulf Hannerz (1996: 89), who claims that such global corporations "may entail a kind and a degree of tuning out, a weakened personal involvement with the nation and national culture, a shift from the disposition to take it for granted; possibly a critical distance to it." In this sense, global corporations are thought to hold the potential for becoming a dominant transnational source of identity; a source of nationally indifferent, global attachments.

On the other hand, many management writers claim that national identities are hardly withering away and are in fact quite persistent and salient in global organizational contexts. Focusing more on behavioral characteristics than on members' sense of belonging, these writers are openly discouraged by the prospects of corporate globalization, laying the blame for repeated international M&As (mergers and acquisitions) failures on persistent identities of members from different national backgrounds. They claim that compared to national M&As, international M&As entail potentially more enhanced intergroup incompatibility and more pronounced intergroup clashes, enhancing the overt and covert hostility that characterize such contexts, and hindering effective consolidations (see Calorie, Lubatkin, and Very 1994; Child, Faulkner & Pitkethly, 2001; Veiga, Lubatkin, Calorie & Very, 2000; Olie, 1994). Concomitantly, managers are warned that the "urge to merge" (Schonfeld 1997) should be balanced by awareness that the blending of two companies may cause a culture clash, marking out identity boundaries that management needs to dissolve, and undermining its efforts to synthesize organizational identities.

This latter view, which speaks of the perpetuation of national identities within the global organization, has also been systematically conceptualized and validated by the field of cross-cultural research.[19] Defining identity as value-based and cognitively constraining (Erez & Earley 1993; Bachrach, Bamberger & Erez 1996), writers in this field claim that national identities persistently manifest themselves in global organizations through patterns of behavior that are distinctive and typical of members' cultures of origin (Hofstede 1980; 1991; 2001). Consequently, in their view, global work-life is marked by a stubborn lack of fit between the behavioral manifestations of cognitively pervasive and unyielding "identity-based systems of interpretation and sense making that the actors involved in these enterprises bring with them" (Bachrach et al. 1996: viii) and the global goals and forms of the organization. In this view, then, the global effort is impeded by the perpetuation of national identities and their manifestation in the behavior of the predetermined selves that are their carriers.

Empirical validation for this view is, for the most part, persuasive.[20] There does seem to be some valid truth and, it might be added, common sense in the claim that Israelis, for example, "act Israeli" or Americans "act American," as well as in the claim that there exists some broadly definable gap in the cognitive underpinnings of such observable behavioral differences. And yet apparently much is missing from this account. As cross-cultural writers conceptualize national identity solely in objectivist and essentialist terms, they fail to take into account the freedom that members have in defining what belongings mean, in shaping identities. [21] For example, when one of the participants in the corporate "wedding" celebration defined his merger partners as "The typical American schmucks, babbling TQM all the time," he seemed to have had some freedom to select and stress certain elements, to reproduce national stereotypes and use them in a certain way. In this sense, he amounted to much more than a passive, static, objectively predetermined, typical Israeli personality: he also appeared to be a constructor, defining and making symbolic use of national identity rather than passively reproducing it. His remark, in other words, illustrates that national identity is not merely an objective essence, but also a flexible and shapeable social construct. Failing to take account of this, cross-cultural researchers seem to fall back on a personality theme that may be valid but is so static and bounded that its relevance to the ongoing social dynamics of everyday global life seems limited.

Another related drawback of cross-cultural and, for that matter, the other, opposing view about organizational globalization is the perception of identity choices as automatic. Whether speaking of the loosening of national identities in global organizations or of their perpetuation, writers holding both of these views conceptualize the problem of identity in terms of a tradeoff between two basic attachments, the national and the global. They promote the assumption that the strengthening of one automatically entails the loosening of the other; that the two are mutually exclusive. The notion of identities' multiple coexistence renders this assumption problematic, as does empirical evidence that indicates that the management of global and national attachments entails tension and demands difficult, far from automatic choices (Mathews 2000). Most strikingly, studies of expatriates and sojourners offer evidence that this management involves complex and ongoing adjustments. National attachments, it is shown, remain meaningful even in the case of those posted at the most extreme international contexts, continuing to coexist alongside the most accelerated cosmopolitan identity projects (Ben-Ari 1996; Thompson & Tambyah 1999; Arieli 2001).

In addition, the assumption of mutual exclusiveness also fails to take into account the fact that other identities are involved in choices that concern global and national identities. In the first merger day event, for example, there was also an appeal to "the workers," a mention of "the senior management team," as well as a reference to the merger partners as occupational colleagues overly preoccupied with TQM. The fact that some of "the typical American schmucks" were also a globally defined "we"—coworkers, co-managers, occupational colleagues—raises many questions: how was this intersection experienced? How did members choose themselves, construct themselves, out of their pool of multiple identities? What were the consequences of their choices?

In sum, in organizations both within the high-tech sector and outside it globalization increasingly blurs the social boundaries within which identities were defined and came to be seen as stable, problematizing them to a great extent. While seeking to evaluate the significance of identities in the global workplace, writings on this topic generally seem to fall short of doing so. Their focus on presumably objective, pen-and-pencil categorizations of identity essences and their conceptualization of global and national identities as mutually exclusive seem a limited and overly simplified orientation to the topic. In contrast to these as well as to the mainstream theoretical orientation toward organizational identity, it has been argued that identities are not single essences but multiple social constructions. Accordingly, a study of them necessitates an inquiry into the everyday global work-life through which they emerge and are enacted. It necessitates going to the people who, in the course of living this global work-life, seek to define, make sense of, and manage their attachments and senses of belonging. A study of identities, in short, should be a study in context.

The Ethnographic Study of Isrocom

The objective of examining identities in context is pursued through an ethnographic study of Isrocom. Ethnography is designed to search for the meanings imputed to the objects of the social worlds that people inhabit (Blumer 1969; Geertz 1973), and is based upon the establishment of close familiarity with the most mundane aspects of everyday life. While to some extent underrepresented in the field of organizational studies or at least in some of its central publication journals (see, for example, Van Maanen 1998b), here too there is growing recognition of the value of the ethnographic method in enabling researchers to grapple with "the specific, always contextual understandings and explanations given by social actors that provide purpose and meaning to their behavior" (Van Maanen 1979b: 12).

The fact that the methodological means fit this study's goals should not be taken to imply that all aspects of the research process were the result of premeditated choices. For one thing, the goals themselves were not predetermined but emergent, their importance and centrality revealed only after fieldwork began. Furthermore, Isrocom was not a deliberate choice. Rather, the decision to study this specific organization was determined by what is perhaps one of the most typical characteristics of ethnographic research in organizational settings: the contingency of access. In my case, it was a lucky constellation of a social network: I was a graduate student at the Department of Labor Studies at Tel Aviv University, a faculty member in my department was acquainted with one of Isrocom's senior executives, and the latter expressed an interest in and consented to allowing a student to conduct research in the organization.

The ethnographic study of Isrocom began on the first day of the merger, January 14th, 1998, and lasted a year. Apart from a standard nondisclosure agreement committing me to secrecy with regard to technological patents and financial data, I was granted a freedom of access. Thanks to a "visitor" tag I was able to enter and wander around the organizational premises freely and independently. During most of the year I used that tag four to five days a week. The exceptions were the months of June, July, and August. During these months my visits to Isrocom were cut down to once a week due to a partial maternity leave.[22]

Despite the tag and the freedom of access (or perhaps because of them), during the initial stages of fieldwork members sometimes expressed apprehensions concerning the purpose of my stay in the field. Asking them for an interview or for permission to observe, I was at times confronted with frank questions about my role. Namely, some members expressed disbelief at my declared lack of organizational status and goal ("Why would managers let you waste the time of so many workers on interviews if there is nothing in it for them?" was the basic argument) and also, after brief interrogations, of my status as a researcher ("What kind of research is it if you don't have hypotheses?"). As a response, I repeatedly assured anyone who asked that I was not in any way a representative of management, that I was merely interested in conducting research, and that I had no intentions of using my research to come up with any managerial prescriptions. After a while, these apprehensions subsided, and it was my impression that members more or less grew accustomed to my presence in the field. Though I doubt that I was ever perceived as "a fly on the wall"—the falsity of this old ethnographic hyperbole is by now widely recognized—I am fairly certain that I was not perceived as an extension of management. It seems to me that I was accepted as a researcher conducting an unusual sort of study with interests that were neutral albeit somewhat unclear.

In the course of my visits to Isrocom I used a variety of fieldwork techniques. To begin with, I conducted formal interviews with members. These interviews were generally in-depth and unstructured, each taking shape as a more or less free-flowing conversation ranging from forty-five minutes to two hours. The interviews usually began with a promise of anonymity, a general statement concerning my interest in studying the merger, and a question or two about the interviewee. After that, I tried to follow whatever topic people wanted to talk about, going along with their line of thought. While I usually tape-recorded the interviews as a way of assuring the validity of the material to be used for analysis, sometimes interviewees requested me not to do so. In such cases I wrote down the conversation while the interview was being conducted, trying very hard not to miss a word.

The selection of interviewees was generally based on a snowballing process. I was not picky: I interviewed anyone willing to talk. I met my interviewees both through chance encounters and through networking: at the end of interviews I asked members if they were willing to give me names of some friends and colleagues with whom I could also talk. The selection of interviewees was also conducted, somewhat more systematically, along the dimension of time. During the second half of the year I conducted several interviews with people that I had interviewed in the first half, in order to trace any changes that might have occurred during the passing time. By the end of the year I had conducted approximately 130 interviews with people from all departments and hierarchical levels.

During my stay in Isrocom I also conducted participant-observations. I invested a great deal of effort in trying to get access to formal events such as training sessions, international conference calls, and work meetings as they occurred across departments, hierarchical levels, and time. After getting myself into some awkward situations, I finally learned that the only way to get access to such events was by asking the permission of the most senior participant, and that the best way to do so was through an interview. Thus interviews became the major vehicle not only for finding potential new interviewees but also for hearing about and getting access to formal events. All of the observations were documented in fieldnotes as they unfolded. Further descriptive elaboration was completed after the event, in order to fill in as much as possible of what was left out due to the pressure of keeping apace with the ongoing interactions.

In between formal interviews and observations I had many free hours. I spent them using a variety of other research techniques. Strolling the corridors of Isrocom, my notebook and pen always with me, I conducted informal interviews in places such as elevators and coffee rooms. I also copied notices from bulletin boards and described practically everything I saw, from the ways members dressed to how they decorated their offices. In addition, I collected documents such as organizational diagrams, personal emails that members were willing to disclose, and invitations to training events. From time to time I sat down in one of the coffee rooms, made myself something warm to drink, and wrote down my own thoughts and feelings about things that I had experienced or encountered or collected during these endless strolls.

By the end of the year I had accumulated thousands of pages of data. After three additional months of transcribing interviews, I finally dedicated my time to the task of "making sense." Basically, this task consisted of three procedures of analysis. The first involved reading and categorization. The fieldnotes were intensively and minutely scrutinized, line by line and word by word, in an attempt to generate, verify, discard, combine, or modify coded groupings. For each of these codes a computer file was then opened, and all of the relevant citations, descriptions, and other bits of information were copied and pasted into it. The material within the files was then read once again and categorized in an attempt to identify underlying themes. During this process, it should be noted, the issue of identity surfaced again and again in various ways. Most significantly, practically every page of the field-notes documented explicit verbal expressions of "us" or "we," or behavioral patterns and physical artifacts that seemed to symbolize attachment to a group: family pictures displayed in the office, the Hebrew spoken among members, wedding rings, men wearing skullcaps, the authoritative tone of managers, and so forth. In the second stage of analysis the identified themes were used to generate hypothetical interpretive frames (Agar 1996) concerning the meaning of identities and their interrelations. The frames were then validated, refuted, or modified through repeated rescannings of the entry files in search of examples, counterexamples, evidence, and exceptions.

The third procedure of analysis was writing. This was a difficult task of forcing it all into a coherently readable format that would most accurately portray the complexity encountered in the field, comply with academic norms and standards of representation, and (nevertheless) avoid as much as possible testing the patience of potential, future readers. It was, in other words, a narration of sorts; a construction of a "tale of the field" (Van Maanen 1988) that lives up to these multiple demands. Moving, as Denzin (1994: 501) calls it, "from field to text to reader" was not a linear process: the tale didn't simply tell itself, and there was a lot of going back and forth between reported facts that had, by this stage, long since passed, and the interpretive representation of them. Turning data into "thick description" (Geertz 1973) was, as qualitative methodologists have long since recognized, a transformative act of inscription (see Denzin 1994; Richardson 1994). Thus, in line with the postmodern climate and the new sensibilities regarding the social scientific text and its claim to authority, this book, I declare, presents my own situated, sense-making interpretation of Isrocom's merger. Grounded in the facts recorded in fieldwork and, furthermore, based upon methodical coding and categorization, this tale that I tell is nevertheless not disembodied, absolute, or exclusive, but a version—my version—of the realities that I observed.

Indeed, as a form of reflexive exercise, it is not difficult to find links between the story that I tell and my own attributes and inclinations. In correspondence to the findings which will soon be reported, my memory of fieldwork is dominated by an internal sense of struggle between two of my own identities: that of a researcher and that of a native-born, Hebrew-speaking Israeli. While many of those who undertake "anthropology at home" often report an experience of "schizophrenia between the 'native self' and 'professional self,'" (Mascarenhas-Keyes 1987: 180) in my case this "schizophrenia" seemed especially poignant. In the context of a merger with Americans, my Israeliness appeared to carry special significance. It seemed to me that members were willing to gloss over that which usually "protects" other home-ethnographers from being completely blinded by familiarity—the foreignness that derives from the very fact of their being ethnographers and thus "neither 'here' nor 'there'" (Hastrup 1987: 105)—and draw me into the neatly emerging categories of "us" versus "them." There was something cozy in this collective embrace, something comforting in the sense of belonging it inspired. In many ways it eased experiences of disorientation and alienation that accompanied this, as any, fieldwork, and countervailed the effects of some of the apprehensions that I was confronted with in my initial interactions in the field.

As I quickly realized, however, it came with a price. Once when discussing some of my field experiences at the university, I caught myself talking as an organizational collective, explaining what "we" in Isrocom are undergoing as part of the merger with "the Americans." I myself was suddenly mobilized, so naturally defining myself as part of the collective that I came to study, realizing through my own experience how compelling is the drive to be a part of and participate in an "us" that is opposed to a "them." The dynamics of polarization, it seems, operated on me too, pressing me into one of its sides.

And yet in my case (as, it will soon be reported, was also the case of the people I studied), polarization was incomplete. While I am Israeli, I was not of the organization. I did, after all, come as a researcher. Practicing this role seemed to have had the effect of distancing me from Isrocom's members and from the experience of "we-ness" with them. The need to document everything, to read the fieldnotes at home in the evenings, to rethink and talk about them at the university, and to engage in detached theoretical reflections somehow made my sense of attachment to Isrocom's members less "real" by turning it into a finding of sorts to be handled externally of the situations that produced it. Adding to this effect was the need to translate: the analysis and writing stages of the research included the translation of data that was collected, for the most part, in Hebrew. Translation too seemed to entail the important benefit of estrangement; of coming to view my drive to be at one with my Isrocom's members in a language different from the one in which it was initially inspired and experienced.[23]

Moreover, not only was I not of the organization in terms of my role and the language of my analysis and writing, I also did not subscribe to a portion of the universe of meaning upon which it was based. Namely, I never actually worked in a high-tech corporation, and, furthermore, have always been critical of profit-seeking corporations and the managerial ideologies that characterize them. Accordingly, during my stay in the field I often found myself bewildered by signs of commitment to organizational demands or ideals (which, as will be reported, were abundant); puzzled by their taken-for-grantedness rather than engulfed by it. Thus, to cite Strathern's (1987: 16) claim about auto-anthropology, "the grounds of familiarity and distance" between the Isrocom's members and myself were "shifting ones." They were to me (as I apparently was to them) both an "us" and a "them." The simultaneous experience of bonds and detachment turned my interactions with them into a constant reminder of my own disjointed multiplicity. Much of what I found in Isrocom's members I had thus found in myself.

This ethnography, in sum, is a specific reading of a specific context. Nevertheless, it is precisely from this situated and local focus that its substantive and theoretical relevance seems to stem. "'Globalization,'" says Bauman (1998:1), "is on everybody's lips; a fad word fast turning into a shibboleth, a magic incantation, a pass-key meant to unlock the gates to all present and future mysteries." One way to make this term less abstract and opaque, is to "ground" globalization (Burawoy 2000): to embark upon ethnographic inquiry into its concrete, local realities and to construct perspectives on it from below. Indeed, Isrocom seems especially valuable in this sense: despite the fact that this company was not a deliberate choice, it does seem to be at least in some respects representative of a significant subset of globalizing organizations, namely local companies undergoing an accelerated process of global expansion. Furthermore, since it belongs to two categories that are claimed to spearhead worldwide processes of globalization, the high-tech sector and multinational corporations,[24] it is possible that the findings reported here will be of relevance to other global contexts as well. A tale of this field, in other words, might inform other tales of other fields. While unable to unlock the gates to all of globalization's mysteries, it can perhaps shed light upon at least some of its everyday realities and underlying complexities.

The Plan of the Study

This study consists of two parts. Each of them deals with a different level of analysis and a different though interrelated objective. The first part is titled "The Merger at Work: Enacting a Separate Organizational Identity in Everyday Life." It consists of detailed, in-depth depictions of two major kinds of interactions that were observed in the field: communication events between members of Isrocom and their merger partners (Chapter 3) and occasions in which Isrocom's members engaged amongst themselves, talking not *to* but *about* their merger partners and referring to various local representations of them (Chapter 4). On the whole, the findings of Part I speak of members' extensive and ongoing, yet paradoxical and incomplete attempts to disengage themselves from the merger partners and sustain a separate local-organizational identity in the face of globalization.

The second part is an inquiry into the consequences of this process of construction for other identities that were experienced in the field. Titled "The Merger and the Worker: Aligning Identities, Centering Selves," it turns to issues of multiplicity and interconnectedness. More specifically, it examines the ways that members perceived and managed the intersection between the separate organizational identity that they continually enacted in the course of everyday work-life and other salient identities that rose to the social fore, namely the Israeli identity (Chapter 5) and work identities (Chapter 6). Based primarily upon an analysis of members' reflections, it shows how these identities were to some degree cast in the mold of the split between Isrocom's "us" and Amerotech's "them," the complex and, at times, ironic and paradoxical constellations of meanings that were involved in this process, and their various effects.

Before turning to the first part of this research, there is a need to set its stage with a more elaborate discussion of the context that was studied. The next chapter, "Setting," is designed for this goal. A backdrop for the study's main two parts, it describes the organizational processes that preceded the merger in Isrocom and presents general information and terms that seem important for the understanding of organizational life in this specific context.

CHAPTER 2

Setting

The Trail to Globalization

Isrocom was a company that designed, developed, manufactured, and marketed a complex telecommunications system called Net. It was founded by three Israelis in a modest apartment in Tel Aviv in the 1980s. According to the founding story that has been repeatedly cited both within Isrocom and in newspaper articles, the founders had global ambitions from the beginning. Isrocom's early years, however, were disappointing. The Israeli economy at the time posed many difficulties for its emergent high-tech sector, inhibiting growth and hindering the materialization of global aspirations. Seeking a breakthrough, the founders established a parent company for Isrocom in the United States in order to increase the likelihood for success within the global arena. They titled it "Com" and issued its stock in the American stock market. By the end of the 1980s the company suffered severe losses, its American stock collapsed, and many workers were fired. Discouraged by the turn of events, two of the founders left.

The rocky start, however, did not seem to weaken global ambitions. For the remaining founder, Dubi R., persistence proved worthwhile. A change in Isrocom's marketing strategy and concomitant technological developments opened new possibilities and produced profits. In the 1990s the company was tremendously prosperous; its growth both rapid and consistent. The product, Net, was purchased by an increasing number of corporate clients throughout the world. It generated the high profits and impressive growth rate that turned Isrocom and its parent company, Com, into favorites of financial analysts and reporters in the international economic community. In Israel the company was typically portrayed as a valued exemplar of a local company that had "made it" in the global market and as a source of national pride. In the mid 1990s it was awarded a special prize by the Israeli government, and both the business and general press affectionately and continually reported the financial figures that had made it one of the few Israeli high-tech companies to attain such eminent international status.

Success spurred further globalization. During the 1990s Isrocom began establishing operational sites and subsidiaries around the world. Accounting for a vast part of the parent company's fortunes, its success provided Com financial strength for a series of acquisitions of several suppliers and minor competitors. In 1997 Dubi R. and a small group of senior managers from Com and Isrocom began negotiating a large merger with Isrocom's fiercest competitor in the global market for almost a decade: Amerotech. This was a New York-based company, similar to Isrocom in size, technology, and market strength. Merger negotiations lasted several months and included crisis-ridden and confidential meetings, at times in secret, private apartments in Manhattan, and several legal dramas. During the summer of 1997 a definitive agreement for a stock-for-stock transaction was signed. It stated that Com's shareholders were to own almost sixty percent and Amerotech's shareholders approximately forty percent of the resulting joint company's stock and that Com's Board of Directors would be expanded to include Amerotech's Chairman and CEO (Chief Executive Officer). In a press release and a voicemail message to the workers, Dubi R. declared that Amerotech would be merged with Com's largest operating unit, Isrocom. Though thus formally defined as a merger, within Isrocom as well as in many newspaper reports, the transaction was often referred to as an Israeli acquisition of an American competitor.

The signing of the definitive agreement marked the beginning of a six-month "waiting period" during which the proposed merger was reviewed for approval by various authorities and the shareholders. Subjected to legal restrictions and the possibility that the merger would not be finalized after all, the two companies continued to operate as separate, competing entities. Nonetheless, some preparations were under way. Senior managers from Isrocom and Amerotech visited each other's premises, and several "Merger Integration Teams" were "kicked off." Each of these teams dealt with a specific topic. For example, the Sales and Marketing Integration Team dealt with product positioning, branding, and exhibition issues; the Human Resources team worked on identifying the top priority joint policies that had to be implemented after the merger; and the R&D Integration Team, unable to reveal technological "secrets" or discuss "real" issues until after the merger's finalization, settled upon the bureaucratic task of designing a future development process for joint projects.

To a great extent, the merger constituted a revolutionary turning point in Isrocom's history. Despite the global scope of its operations and achievements, until the merger the company was predominantly Israeli. Most strikingly, although some of its one thousand employees were from foreign countries (including a few Americans in an office in Albany), the vast majority of workers and managers, including senior managers, were Israelis living in Israel. Furthermore, the entire R&D and manufacturing operations were located in Tel Aviv. Even marketing and customer-support activities, both global in scope, were managed from Isrocom's local headquarters, and, for the most part, performed by Israeli workers living in Israel or aboard. Despite the global ambitions, Isrocom was thus, for the most part, a local company. To use the words of one of its top managers, its aim was "to be like Ericsson: a company from a small country that conquers the global market."[1]

When I first visited the company at the end of 1997, working out the details of the upcoming fieldwork, this blending of global ambitions and a local 'heart' was very pronounced. Isrocom was located in Tel Aviv, in a once run-down industrial park that is increasingly taken over by new, modern buildings of high-tech corporations. Driving through the park, it was hard not to notice Isrocom's facilities. They were among the more impressive in the area: tall and shiny, reflecting a bright world through their large windows and glass-coated walls. Entering the main building, an endless variety of artifacts bore evidence to the company's Israeliness, from the blue and white logo of 'Isrocom' that was exhibited at the entrance,[2] to the Hebrew chatter of the receptionists. Yet the first thing that caught my attention was a large logo that hung above the reception desk, spelling out the company's global title, 'Com,' in gold-colored letters. Inside the building, employees hurried through long, narrow corridors wearing tags that displayed their Hebrew names in English letters, binding their most personal token of local identity to the language of the world. As they passed, their quiet Hebrew talk could be heard, along with surprisingly loud and patently anxious Israeli-accented English that occasionally came out of small offices or open-space cubicles where members talked to a distant customer or supplier on the phone. On bulletin boards on every floor, Hebrew notices from the Human Resource department hung next to shiny English fliers with pictures of foreign places, inviting participation in upcoming exhibitions or professional conferences. During my visit, I ran into a group of clients from abroad that was escorted through these premises. The foreignness of these clients stood out and was as evident to me as the eagerness with which they were catered to by their hosts. Through such sights, sounds, and scenes, both the company's local Israeli character and global commitment emerged as a strongly felt reality.

The merger, however, marked a new, more sophisticated form of global adventure. In Globalint, the merged corporate entity, Isrocom's local population barely amounted to a half of the total employee population; its work processes and hierarchy were spread across the ocean; and it lost its superiority and exclusiveness as headquarters that set a dominant local tone to worldwide operations. This time, globalization reached deep, challenging the local organization's internal character, structure, and standing. Now, it was to determine not only what the organization does—its operational goals and ambitions—but also what the organization is, its internal quality and formal identity.

Nevertheless, in press releases and in letters to customers, this turning point was portrayed as a natural development in both of the merger partners' organizational life cycles. According to the business rationale that was repeatedly cited, the two companies jointly held a substantial market share consisting of complementary business and territorial segments. Moreover, the two companies produced competing products, and the possibility of combining their R&D capabilities was said to imply heightened professional expertise. With combined market strength and engineering expertise, the merged entity, "Globalint," was destined to become a world leader in its field. The merger was thus depicted as the next logical step in the process of globalization, offering management an opportunity to take advantage of the best economic possibilities that existed in both organizational worlds.

Internally, management's rhetoric combined excitement toward a changing future with commitment to preserving much of the past. "I am personally excited about this merger," the CEO from Amerotech wrote in an official merger announcement letter to the new international mixture of subordinates, promising "exciting opportunities for the future as we expand our technologies and resources." In the spirit of merger, the Israeli COO "mirrored his words," adding a request "to roll up your sleeves and share your technical and product recommendations and insight during the challenging months ahead." Additionally, senior management also attempted to assure workers that this organizational marriage of sorts implied minimal changes in their work-lives. Answering "Merger Questions" that members were encouraged to send through the email, they promised continuity in relation to matters such as corporate spirit ("The new organization will continue to uphold goals and values we both currently support," "Our goal is to continue to keep the spirit of a small company in a much larger organization"); conduct ("We plan to continue development and production of both product lines," "We expect to continue manufacturing in both locations"); job security ("We expect to continue to expand our workforce with no reduction of current employee population"); and rewards ("All Com stock and stock options plans will remain unchanged").

The merger did, however, introduce significant changes to everyday life. In order to provide a general background and introduce organizational terms and concepts that will be referred to later in the analysis, the following sections outline the major transformations that were introduced.

Merging Management

The formal merger chart **(Figure 1)** was designed by the architects of the merger (Dubi R., the CEOs of Amerotech and Isrocom, and several Executive Vice Presidents from both sides) and published during its initial stages. As it indicates, the senior management team included two hierarchical levels: the first consisted of the Chief Executive and Operations Officers (CEO and COO) and the second of Executive Vice Presidents and Vice Presidents (EVPs and VPs). The higher level was formally shared by the prior CEOs of Amerotech and Isrocom. While the former was titled CEO of Globalint and the latter COO, their relationship was not a hierarchical reporting relationship, but merely a formal division of labor: the American CEO was made responsible for marketing and strategy, and the Israeli COO for technology and operations. Throughout the year of study, however, the COO took over many of the formal responsibilities of his American counterpart. Increasingly, he seemed to have become the center of decision making and authority in Globalint. Concomitantly, members often referred to his inferior title as a form of lip service to those acquired; a means for lifting their morale. The rumor that spread toward the end of the year was that the American CEO was on his way to an early retirement.

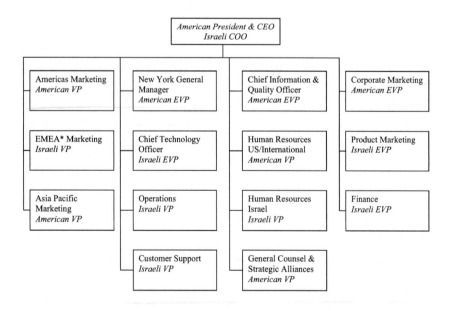

* EMEA – Europe, Middle East, Australia

Figure 1. *Globalint's Merger Chart*

The lower ranks of the senior management team consisted of Vice Presidents (VPs and EVPs) in positions of department heads.[3] In their case, the formal division of labor between Isrocom's and Amerotech's managers was more clear-cut than that between the CEO and COO. Almost every pair of parallel departments was combined under a single manager. Thus only one of every Israeli and American counterparts remained in position. As **Figure 1** indicates, it seems that there was a deliberate effort to ensure that exactly half the managers in this level were from Isrocom and half from Amerotech. Among the local managers who had to leave their positions, several took a different position and several left. No one, however, was explicitly notified of being laid off. There were more implicit strategies for letting some of these managers know that they were no longer needed. These included offering them a new position that marked a demotion or appointing them to act as instructors-of-sorts for their American inheritors with the evasive promise that within six months a new position would probably pop up.

The merging of the lower rank of senior management created an unusual turbulence. Most of Isrocom's senior managers had been with the organization for several years, and, at least since Isrocom's historic transition from failure to success in the beginning of the 1990s, their hierarchical climb was relatively smooth, sustained by the mere growth of the organization. "Isrocom's managers," one told me, "did not climb up to the ceiling: rather, the floor dropped further and further down below their feet." Though there were, to be sure, political issues that high-level managers had to tend to while securing their status, the merger did seem to add confusion and uncertainty to what was otherwise a milder political arena.

Yet even for those who survived the turbulence of the managerial selection, the merger often implied a problematic turning point in their professional lives. Generally, managers in Isrocom (as elsewhere in the high-tech sector) were assessed by their ability to motivate subordinates to complete assignments with tight time frames or "impossible deadlines" (the eternal, hysteria-ridden slips included); to extract as much as possible out of as few "man-hours" as possible. Running from one meeting to the next, they were mostly busy securing and coordinating the time and effort of their subordinates: defining their schedules, distributing and monitoring assignments, obtaining the budgetary and technological means necessary for motivating them to contribute, buffering them against organizational disturbances and distractions, and so forth. With the merger, life became much more hectic and pressures heightened as their responsibilities widened to include American subordinates as well. In addition to their usual duties in Tel Aviv came the intricate task of assuming the duties of the "dethroned" Amerotech manager. Trips abroad grew frequent and "inter-cultural skills" were deemed increasingly important for finding one's way and mastering an entirely new organizational universe with its own processes and procedures, practices and perspectives.

For some of these managers, the merger also implied a change in the relationship with their superiors. As the organization and their own duties multiplied, many of them suddenly found themselves removed from the center of decision-making. Complaining about "the crumbling of the decision making circle" or "the loss of a sense of consensus," such managers realized that they had drifted away from the locus of power and authority. Nonetheless, since this locus quickly appeared to be dominated by the local COO and his assistants rather than by the American CEO, many of them took comfort in the claim that they were still better off than their colleagues from abroad. They had more to bind them to those on top: a space that allowed one to bump into and socialize with her/his seniors in the hallway, a past that offered one familiarity and a plethora of bonding memories with decision makers, and a national identity that gave one a language in relation to which the organizationally powerful could feel at home. "It is very plausible," said one manager after counting these exclusively local advantages, "that Amerotech's managers will not survive."

Merging Products

Isrocom and Amerotech produced two competing telecommunications products. While fulfilling the same function, the two products differed in several respects and each was equipped to serve a different kind of client. In addition, at the time of the merger each was already owned by a large number of clients. Accordingly, senior management decided not to merge these existing products. Both of them continued to be manufactured and supported by each site, and new clients were offered the product that suited them best.

Though it lasted the entire year, this arrangement was nonetheless presented as temporary. Strategically, the two existing products were to remain separate only until a unitary future product would replace them. The nature of that unitary future product, however, was difficult to determine. In fact, it became one of the major sources of contention in the first post-merger months. Isrocom's engineers, on one hand, sought to defend the years of work that they had put into developing a revolutionary future product practically from scratch. They passionately argued for the need to continue with their work. Amerotech's engineers, on the other hand, promoted an "evolutionary" strategy of designing unitary, incremental "add-ons" to the existing products. Overruling local objection, management ultimately chose Amerotech's technical perspective. However, its decision did not put an end to the contention. What quickly became titled "The Not Invented Here War" went on: there seemed to have been a great unwillingness on the side of the local engineers to accept the technology and ideas of Amerotech. While some progress was achieved, it was significantly less than was expected. By the end of the year, the Chief Technology Officer admitted that the company was yet unsuccessful in overcoming "the engineering ego" and the "emotional issues" related to technology.

Merging Departments

In the few weeks after the merger was finalized, almost every one of Isrocom's geographical and functional departments issued a new merger-chart. These charts were themselves something of a novelty. Insiders often took pride in the claim that before the merger, Isrocom's departments managed to sustain the informal, flat-hierarchy spirit of start-ups despite their growing size. The status of formal charts was consistent with this view: they lacked specifications of status titles, were difficult to come by, and were fashionably dismissed as an inadequate description of an informal, ambiguous, and constantly changing organizational reality. In contrast, the new merger charts were specific with regard to status titles, they were widely published, and, most interestingly, they were hardly dismissed as irrelevant: after the merger, the formal structure was no longer viewed as a problematic or inferior tool for the description of a complex organizational reality, but rather as a powerful tool for its construction. Anxiously awaiting their publication and at times boldly contesting their content, many seemed to view these designs as a primary indication of their position of power vis-à-vis the new, global work processes.

The structural transformations themselves were diverse. While almost every one of Isrocom's departments was merged with its American counterpart, each of these mergers took a distinct form. In what follows, I summarize the major departmental mergers that were instituted in Globalint, ordered according to the company's underlying work process: sales by Marketing, customized development by R&D, production by Operations, and support by Customer Support. A final section specifies the merger of the two major staff departments: Finance and Human Resources.[4]

Marketing

Within Isrocom, three geographical marketing departments—Asia Pacific, EMEA (Europe, Middle East, Australia), and Americas—and one functional marketing department—Product Marketing[5]—were responsible for securing business deals with clients. The three geographical departments were fairly autonomous and self-sufficient units, each handling sales in a different segment of the world. Product Marketing dealt with centralized marketing functions, such as new product planning, product training, and marketing support programs.

The marketing departments employed three major kinds of workers. The first two were somewhat peripheral in status: young secretaries, all of them women, who provided administrative services; and pre-sale people, often subcontracted abroad, who made first contacts with clients and helped support the sales. The third kind of workers were the marketing engineers or "project managers." Seen by many as the company's "combat fighters" and "money makers," these were ambitious technical professionals, often with prior engineering and R&D experience, who had made a much sought-after career move into marketing, usually after the completion of an MBA. Despite the frequent trips abroad and intense work pressure, their role was one of the most prestigious in the company, involving considerable financial and status rewards. Though they lacked direct subordinates ("managers without soldiers"), they constituted the origin of most of the company's internal work processes. Focusing on a small number of clients from a single region or country, each of them was responsible not only for "making sales" but also for "moving things" within the organization; for coordinating and monitoring all the different organizational processes necessary to make deliveries on time.

The merger entailed significant structural transformations for marketing. While Product Marketing remained hierarchically separate in all but a joint department head (from Isrocom), each of the geographical departments was integrated with its parallel at all levels of hierarchy: Isrocom's Americas Department was subordinated to the head of Amerotech's larger and more successful Americas Department, and integrated into its existing hierarchy; Amerotech's EMEA Department was subordinated to the head of Isrocom's larger and more successful EMEA Department and integrated into its existing structure; and in the case of Asia Pacific, Isrocom's and Amerotech's departments were both completely restructured, and a new, globally zigzagging hierarchy with alternating Israeli and American levels was established and headed by the manager from New York. Moreover, in all departments, including Product Marketing, many of the work processes were integrated. Thus, members were required to continually exchange information about clients, pricing strategies and offers, market news, planning, training, and so forth, and also to coordinate activities on a routine basis.[6]

Research and Development

Two separate research and development (R&D) units operated within Isrocom. The main R&D unit, Net1 R&D, consisted of young engineers and computer programmers. Among them were many permanent employees and a few freelancers.[7] All members of Net1 R&D worked long hours in order to meet the deadlines and demands of dozens of "projects." These, generally, were customized Net-features that their colleagues from Marketing demanded for customers. Since Net was a large and relatively old system, a significant portion of the professional work in this R&D unit was seen as "patch work" or even "dirty work" involving unattractive and, in some cases, outdated technology. Accordingly, the main aspirations of ambitious, career-oriented engineers and programmers who worked in this unit seemed to concern positions having more to do with management than with technology. The first rung of the managerial ladder was that of "team leader": a position with responsibility for coordinating and taking care of the requirements of small project groups of three to ten members.

Structurally, Net1 R&D consisted of three regional software project groups. Each of them was budgeted by and connected through matrix "dotted lines" to the parallel regional marketing department. Furthermore, Net1 R&D also consisted of additional functional groups such as generic software development, hardware, and testing groups. Since it was decided that Net would continue to be developed and maintained in the merged organization, many R&D employees seemed to be minimally affected by the merger. Nonetheless, there were several significant transformations here too. Namely, various team leaders and group managers had to maintain contact with counterparts from Amerotech in order to exchange technological information; a new group was established for coordinating and working with New York engineers on the development of the unitary interface and "add-ons"; and several work processes and procedures were united, such as those related to quality control and product testing.

The second Israeli R&D unit was named Net2 R&D. This was a small, confidential, and prestigious unit. Its sole responsibility was to design Isrocom's future product from scratch using the most advanced technology available. As a consequence of management's decision to adopt Amerotech's "evolutionary" strategy after the merger, this acclaimed unit lost the justification for its separate existence. After several months of uncertainty and turmoil, its manager quit his job, and it was annexed to the main Net1 R&D unit, albeit with some degree of managerial and administrative separateness. Its members began working closely with Net1 R&D engineers, assisting them with the development of technologically advanced features and "add-ons."

Operations

Isrocom's Operations Department was responsible for manufacturing Net systems as well as for maintaining the facilities and organizational information technology (IT) systems. Its population was quite heterogeneous, consisting of diverse occupations: industrial engineers in managerial roles and in the Production Engineering Group, technicians in the Production Group, economists in the Planning Group, computer programmers in the IT Group, buyers in the Purchasing Group, and exporters in the Export Group. Here too, as in most places within Isrocom, work was dominated by heavy workloads and strict deadlines. Nonetheless, there did appear to be something exceptional about the work atmosphere in Operations, perhaps a consequence of the tight disciplinary practices on the shop floor, the constant managerial concern with standardization, rationalization, and efficiency maximization, and other such attributes that seemed to have turned this department into one reminiscent of industrial organizations in a high-tech context. In addition, members of the Operations department often complained about a low status attributed to them in the organization. Occupationally, many felt that their jobs were considered peripheral in relation to those of the core high-tech.

Though Isrocom and Amerotech both continued to manufacture their company's original products after the merger, both companies' Operations departments were subordinated to a joint senior management team from Tel Aviv. While there were persistent rumors that Amerotech's production floor will be transferred to Israel, this did not happen during the year that was studied. Structurally, the two departments remained separate below the level of senior management. Nevertheless, workers were made responsible for cooperation and continual exchange of information through email, routine reports, and weekly conference call meetings. In some of the Operations departments' functional groups, for example in Purchasing and Planning, work processes were united and joint teams were defined for tasks such as designing price-offers, negotiating with suppliers, and planning.

Customer Support

After a Net system was sold by Marketing, its customized features developed by R&D and its hardware produced by Operations, it was shipped to a customer. From that point on, the system was generally under the responsibility of the Customer Support Department. This department offered technical support services throughout the world. Dealing solely with actual (rather than potential) customers, it was responsible for installing, maintaining, and upgrading Net systems, as well as for providing training and consultation to systems' owners. Since calls for support services were usually urgent, demanding an immediate response, Customer Support had operational sites located around the world, and the first levels ("tiers") of support services were offered by these sites' local "Field Service Engineers."

Most of the managers and those considered "the experts," however, worked in the headquarters at Tel Aviv. Since field problems often persisted, quickly escalating to higher support "tiers," the work of these managers and experts demanded maximum availability. It was not unusual for a member of this department to receive urgent telephone calls in the middle of the night or to be asked to fly, on a few hours notice, to customer sites around the world. Accordingly, the core population of the department consisted of young, single technicians or engineers with an ability and a desire to travel the world.

The formal structure of the department consisted of three geographical groups (Americas, EMEA, Asia-Pacific), as well as several functional groups dealing with internal departmental services such as training and expert assistance. After the merger, the various groups within the department were integrated to significant degrees[8] and the entire department was subordinated to a VP from Isrocom. Moreover, here too there were cases of joint work projects and teams as well as a continual requirement to make routine updates and exchange information and knowledge about the products, clients, and professional issues such as support procedures and training.

Staff

There were two major staff departments within Isrocom: Finance and Human Resources. The former was a small and very busy department consisting of economic analysts working directly with senior management. After the merger, Amerotech's department was subordinated to Isrocom's department head and work processes were united to a substantial degree. These merged work processes demanded tight cooperation and ongoing exchange of information.

In contrast to Finance and, for that matter, all of the other departments, Isrocom's and Amerotech's Human Resource (HR) departments remained almost completely separate, lacking even a joint department head. According to the VP of HR, the decision to maintain two separate HR organizations resulted from "the importance of the local element" in human resource management. While there was a need to coordinate HR's work processes and procedures in order to assure a minimal degree of organizational unity, there was a greater need to maintain local expertise. After all, Isrocom and Amerotech operated within different labor markets characterized by different rules and norms. Thus, all HR functions—recruitment, compensation, training, placement, welfare—were left separate. Nonetheless, both HR departments had to maintain close contact and continually exchange information, and there were often joint teams that were organized for specific projects such as the organization of joint training events, the issuing of a new employee appraisal form, or the unification of the travel policy.

Merging Communication

The merger between Isrocom and Amerotech also included the integration of internal communication processes. This task consisted of three major elements. First, information technologies were united. Indeed, in the initial stages of the merger the integration of the technological infrastructures was considered a high-priority corporate task. "It was immediately understood that we have to overcome the distance between the two companies," a manager from the Information Technology (IT) group in Operations told me, "and though it is impossible to do so in a physical sense, it is possible to do so in a virtual sense." Accordingly, an IT integration team was one of the first merger-teams to be formed. Working under the focus and attention of senior management, its goal was to make the technology not only available but also "transparent" to users. This meant that the IT integration team was responsible for ensuring that the technological means of working and communicating between the two sites would be identical in terms of user interface to the means of working and communicating within each site. Stated differently, the IT team was responsible for making the technological networks indiscriminate of place.

"Transparency" was accomplished on various fronts. To begin with, the telephony system was programmed to enable a four-digit instead of a nine-digit dial between Tel Aviv and New York. Consequently, it took the same amount of dialing for an Israeli to talk to a coworker in New York as it did for an Israeli to talk to a coworker in Tel Aviv. Additionally, "transparency" was also accomplished with regard to several computer systems and networks. From the first week of the merger, organizational members were able to exchange written messages and attachment files through a combined email system, with the help of a united, computerized email address list. Several months after the merger, a computerized scheduler was implemented in both sites, enabling easy calculations of and adjustment to the seven hours' time difference. In addition, Amerotech's intranet—an internal information network—was installed in Tel Aviv. Though several of the intranet's information sites were completed or added on only later in the year, many sites were available from the beginning. One of them was a joint, alphabetically ordered member list, complete with the role title, telephone numbers, email address, and smiling photograph of each employee.[9]

The second element in the merger of communication processes was the institution of communication events. These consisted of weekly conference calls; the less frequently held "kickoff," semiannual, and business meetings; and, finally, joint trainings. In such events, members from the two sites gathered at a certain time, and, with the exception of conference calls, at a certain place, in order to coordinate and adjust integrated work processes. During the limited time spans that they took place, such events complemented the merged structures with what they basically lacked: coexistent and synchronous temporal and spatial expressions.

Third, management sought to remove obstacles from and create channels for intersite information flows. Thus, in the initial merger phase, the various merger integration teams created "common language definitions" as a means for insuring that important terms such as "urgent," "likely," or "critical" would mean the same at both sites and that the often-used three-letter acronyms would be shared. The teams also defined common time frames, exchanged mapped diagrams of internal work processes and procedures, and selected "contact points": members who acted as channels of information helping people from the other site find their way among those of their own.

Merging "Cultures"

Management's dealings with what was often referred to as "the cultural gap" were based on a perceived distinction between two kinds of cultures. "It was obvious to us from the beginning," claimed a senior HR manager, "that we are identifying two kinds of cultural differences: one is Israelis versus Americans and the other is Amerotech as a company versus Isrocom as a company."

Management attempted to monitor and manage these two "cultural gaps" in significantly different ways. In the initial stages of the merger, the perceived gap between the two organizational cultures—"Amerotech as a company versus Isrocom as a company"—was rhetorically presented as minimal. "After spending time together," it was stated on the "Merger Questions" document that was distributed through the email, "it is clear that our business models and cultures are far more similar than ever imagined." Senior managers spoke of "incredible commonalities," "similar values and work ethics," and "twin hard-working and aggressive spirits." Seeking "scientific proof" for these claims, the "Cultural Integration Team" conducted a "Cultural Assessment" survey among a random selection of about 60 employees from both sites. "Company culture is known as a major topic in mergers," it was stated on the survey's front page, and a survey is needed in order "to help us to assess the similarities and differences between the two companies." Survey participants were asked to rank their agreement with twenty-one positively worded statements concerning various valued characteristics of their "company's culture," and to prioritize the statements that they "feel are imperative for the success of your company."[10] Analyzing the results, the team calculated the average ranking of agreement per statement for each company separately, and then compared them as an indication of a "gap." Similar averages were celebrated (even when both averages were low), and the team happily reported that "The findings were most interesting: employees of both companies perceive the company culture in almost the same way."

Nevertheless, the team did recommend some "action items." These items referred to highly prioritized survey statements with relatively high average-gaps. Basically, the "action items" spoke of the need to implement the managerial practices of the company that "scored more favorably" on each gap-indicating statement in the new merged company. Thus, referring to a statement on which Amerotech "scored more favorably," the team recommended the implementation of its reward and recognition programs. In reference to statements in which Isrocom "scored more favorably," it recommended the introduction of "an orderly practice of long term planning," "a new combined performance appraisal process," and the incorporation of "a value that speaks to the importance of creative solutions that are opportunistic as well as a value that speaks to the issue of flexibility to our customers and prospective customers." Thus, the "Cultural Integration Team" sought to methodically identify the degree that members of the two merged organizations had experienced the same valued corporate attributes, and, in cases of dissimilar degrees of professed experience, the team recommended the homogenization of practices.

Thus it seems that here too, as in the case of the technological merger, management sought "transparency." It sought to homogenize employees' cultural interface, so to speak, with the company, to make organizational culture indiscriminate of place by implementing identical managerial practices in places where such interfaces seemed to diverge. It should be stressed, however, that the implementation of the cultural "transparency" strategy was limited and slow as compared to that of the technology. For example, during the year of study only one of Amerotech's recognition policies ("The Achievers' Club") and one of its reward policies ("Employee Stock Purchase Plan") were implemented in Isrocom months after the merger was finalized and with substantial variations from the American originals.

Management's orientation to the second gap that it identified, the proclaimed difference existing between the Israeli and American national cultures, was significantly different than its orientation to the organizational-culture gap. While managers considered organizational culture to be manageable, they viewed national culture as something beyond their control. When it comes to Israelis versus Americans, managers stated in interviews, it is impossible to bridge the gap. Accordingly, management's efforts were not directed toward the goal of diminishing differences between Israeli and American employees, but rather toward the goal of minimizing possible friction in cross-cultural work interactions. Thus said the senior HR manager:

We don't want to make the Americans change and I don't want to change the Israelis. I don't believe in this . . . We don't intend to turn New Yorkers into Israelis
and the Israelis into New Yorkers, but to allow multiple cultures to co-exist. . . .
It seems to me both an unwise and a farfetched idea to think that you can simply
decide on culture X. . . . The goal is to develop sensitivity and patience to the
multiplicity of cultures. . . . What we can do in this regard is to set some minimal standards or rules of a game that must be accepted. If I know that when I do
this or that it angers you, then I won't do this or that.

This strategy for dealing with the national culture—setting "some
minimal standards or rules of a game"—was systematically implemented
through "Cross-Cultural Workshops." These workshops were conducted
by a consultant about once a month, each time with a different audience
consisting of around two dozen participants who worked with New York.
The goal of these workshops, according to the consultant, was to promote
communication between the merger partners, and ensure that the American partners of interaction would not "become offended," "be scared off,"
or "get mad" when interacting with Israelis in ways that would impair the
merger effort. Accordingly, the participants were asked, for example, to be
polite, to refrain from being pushy, aggressive, or direct, and to stick to formal rules of interaction including "when you meet an American you say
'Hi,' and then you introduce yourself, and then you say 'Nice to meet you.'"
These "minimal standards or rules of a game" were also asserted through
management's scolding of inappropriate behavior. Consider, for example,
the following email from the Israeli COO:

Subject: Negative Feedback from Amerotech Employees
To: All Isrocom Management

I have received some negative feedback from New York employees related to behavior of Isrocom people visiting New York. Please see as follows:

1. On several occasions at New York's office, Isrocom employees have been heard
conversing in Hebrew in the presence of Amerotech employees. While it is per-
fectly understandable that it is easier and more efficient to converse in one's native tongue, be aware that it can create feelings of exclusion, estrangement and
paranoia among the Amerotech people.

2. Certain Isrocom employees visiting New York have used the offices of traveling
Amerotech employees (without prior permission) to make phone calls, etc. This
can (and apparently has) been viewed as a presumptuous violation of personal
space, and should be avoided.

Please give your people appropriate instructions so as to avoid similar instances
in the future.

To summarize, management's cultural strategy was twofold. With regard to the "organizational-culture gap," management sought to implement the cultural parallel of the technological transparency strategy. Rhetorically, it celebrated similarities. Practically, it attempted to diminish perceived differences by homogenizing practices. With regard to the "national-culture gap," management acknowledged its inability to achieve transparency in the same way. Instead, Israeli employees were required to foster an impression of 'transparency' in their interactions with Americans by adhering to an explicit set of performance rules.

Summary

Isrocom's merger with Amerotech marked a revolutionary change in its history. Though the company had always sought global status and was also quite successful at achieving it, up to the time of the merger it was still predominantly local. The decision to unite the structure and work processes of this successful high-tech company, its fortune and destiny, with a competitor located halfway around the world, implied a notably new stage of globalization.

The transformations that were introduced as a consequence of the merger were extensive. After some political turmoil, the management team on each side was downsized and then integrated with its counterpart. For those who remained in their positions, merger reality implied a widened scope of responsibility and accompanying difficulties with respect to both subordinates and superiors. As far as the two products were concerned, the merger included the unification of the strategic product plan. While both of the original products were maintained, there were intensive and at times clashing efforts to design a unitary future product, and these efforts eventually led to the closing of Isrocom's Net2 R&D organization.

Various changes were also introduced by the merger of departments, communication flows, and "cultures." Broadly, each of the geographical and functional departments was in some ways united with its parallel in Amerotech. At times this meant the mere demand for information exchange and cooperation, while at other times it involved complete reorganization. Examined from members' points of view, the departmental mergers entailed different kinds of formal positions vis-à-vis the internationally crosscutting structure. In every merged department members were subsequently situated at new and divergent positions of hierarchical power relative to the merger partners: as superiors, as subordinates, as parallels, as combinations of all of these. This international matrix of formal power was further accompanied by the "transparent" integration of communication systems, the institutionalization of communication events, the standardization of work terms, and the appointment of contact points. Finally, there were also attempts to forge a fit both between the two organizational cultures and between the two national cultures.

In all these ways, the merger constituted a major structural and social turning point for Isrocom. It entailed the unification and integration of multiple dimensions of the formal organization. How did members react to these transformations? How did they make sense of them? How did they construct a sense of belonging, an organizational identity, in the face of them? Seeking to explore these questions, we now turn to the analysis of the merger at work. We undertake an inquiry into the realities of everyday merger life in Isrocom.

PART I

The Merger at Work: Enacting a Separate Organizational Identity in Everyday Life

CHAPTER 3

Identity and Communication Events

Facing the Merger Partners in Person

The encounter with others, claims Barth (1969) in his classic *Ethnic Groups and Boundaries,* is foundational of identity.[1] In contrast to "the naive assumption that each tribe and people has maintained its culture through a bellicose ignorance of its neighbors," he says, and in contrast to "the simplistic view that geographical and social isolation have been the critical factors in sustaining cultural diversity," (1969: 9) identity becomes meaningful at its boundaries. At points of intergroup encounters, notions of uniqueness and belonging are asserted, validated, and maintained. Accordingly, at such points of encounter we embark upon the study of identity in Isrocom.

Inside the merged corporation, intergroup engagements took the form of "communication events": occasions during which members from Isrocom and Amerotech engaged in an actual dialogue with each other, usually as a means for exchanging information and coordinating activities. Their routine work-lives physically confined to their respective local sites, members used global technology to communicate with colleagues and peers from abroad. On relatively rare occasions involving trans-Atlantic travel, members also engaged in face-to-face meetings.

In what follows, I offer accounts of both technologically mediated and face-to-face communication events. In order to capture the dynamics of the naturally evolving identity-construction process, the events are described as they unfolded and my interpretations are woven into and flow along with them. My intent is not to blur but rather to bring to light the inevitable complexity, the unexpected twists and incoherent turns of the social processes that are described. This chapter thus presents undivided, extensive, and contextualized glimpses into the actual workings of the globalized Isrocom.

Technologically Mediated Communication Events

The common form of communication between members of Isrocom and Amerotech was technologically mediated. For everyday work matters, as well as for regular work meetings, members made use of the merged technological infrastructure to contact their merger partners abroad. Two major kinds of technologies were used for these purposes: the telephone and the email. Illustrative of each, this section offers accounts of a conference call and an email exchange. The two accounts are followed by a comparative discussion that analyzes their main findings.

Backstage on Line: A Conference Call

It was four p.m. when I walked into the small office of Merav, a member of a team from Product Marketing. She and her boss, Eytan, invited me to observe a conference call with teammates from New York, and the call was about to begin. Merav was working on her laptop and talking on the phone simultaneously, and it took her several seconds to realize that I was standing at the door. When she finally looked up and saw me, she whispered "Hi," and added, "Is it four already? Damn." Getting up, she told the person on the phone, "I'm really sorry, I've got a conference call with the Americans now. I've got no patience for it now, but I have to go." The joint team had not yet assembled, and its meeting not yet begun, but the boundaries that sliced through it were already invoked. Uttering "the Americans," Merav represented team members from Amerotech in terms of a broad national type, permeating the definition of the conference-call situation with a sense of a solid, externally determined distinction. She also rendered whoever was on the phone (and myself) as a member who belonged to her non-American side and as someone who, by virtue of this belonging, was allowed a view of her "real" feelings toward the upcoming team event. Her utterance, incidental and fleeting as it may seem, served as prelude to all that was about to pass.

After I picked Merav up from her office, we walked together to the spacious office of the EVP of Product Marketing, who was currently abroad. There was a round table in the office, and placed in its center was a triangular speakerphone. Four engineers from R&D who had been invited to take part in the call in order to offer information and "stay in the loop" were already seated at the table, discussing a technical matter. "Hi"s were exchanged, and Merav dialed a long number on the phone. Her boss, Eytan, answered the call from a Parisian airport where he was waiting for a flight home. Again referring to the teammates in terms of their nationality, he said, "I am the first one here, the Americans are not on line yet." Alex, one of the engineers, turned to me and jokingly bolstered the boundary: "Write this down, write this down," he said, "even the Americans are late." Anat, Merav's teammate, entered the room, and, as if recognizing some joint social face, joined in and asked: "No one from New York? We're still talking Hebrew, right?" The Hebrew-speaking "we" was thus asserting its defining distinctiveness from the American merger partners, reaffirming itself while waiting for the call to begin.

With its boundaries established, the team then turned to formulating a collective position toward the upcoming event. Udi, an engineer, turned to Merav and asked, "Are we planning to talk to them about the internet issue or is this of no interest to them?" Merav answered his question in the same boundary-setting vein. "It does not interest them," she said, defining rules for the upcoming intergroup interaction, "don't even mention it during the call." "Then what should we tell them?" Udi asked, seeking more specific guidance and further strengthening the sense of collective action. "Should we talk about the platforms because they cannot be connected to our product?" Turning to the triangular speakerphone, Merav asked Eytan for his thoughts on the matter, but before he could answer, the phone beeped. Heads turned to face the phone, and a foreign voice filled the room: "Hello? Who is there?" Suddenly, almost unexpectedly, a technological curtain had been lifted and the group was "on the air."

"We are all here at the Tel Aviv site," Merav spoke first, "except for Eytan, who is talking from Paris. Who is there at your site?" Another voice listed the names, identified himself as "Mark," and then began discussing the first issue on an agenda that had been prepared and distributed ahead of time. As he spoke, everyone in the room was silent for a while, all eyes looking down at the speakerphone. Then, just as swiftly as the technological curtain had been raised, a social curtain was lowered: Merav looked up, and, through pantomime gestures, exhibited to all those present in the room that she did not understand what Mark was saying. She bent over to Tziki, an engineer who was seated next to her, and whispered to him in Hebrew: "What are they talking about?" Tziki pressed the phone's mute button, and explained to her what "they" wanted. A backstage (Goffman, 1959) was thus constructed through the pantomime gestures, the Hebrew whispers, and the use of the mute button. It was confined to the concrete walls of the room, to its physical space, and it rendered the teammates from New York outsiders once again. When Mark finished talking, Eytan, from his distant Parisian location, said, "It is fine with me. Let's hear what Merav is thinking." Singled out of the local group, all eyes upon her, Merav smiled, amused. "Tziki, what do *you* think?" she cynically passed it on, demonstrating her allegiance to the assumption of collectivity. "Okay," Tziki smilingly answered. They were acting in unison and apparently enjoying it. Boundaries were being redefined, and a sense of oneness seemed to fill the participants within them.

As the conversation flowed on, Liz from New York asked more technical questions. Her questions inspired a round of Hebrew whispers: group members were exchanging information and coordinating their reply. They were self-consciously assembling and adjusting a concerted social face. Furthermore, through their whispering they also seemed to be challenging the speakerphone, disputing its technological prowess in dismantling social and physical boundaries. The challenge was magnified when, for several seconds, the connection was disturbed by odd noises. Liz's words sounded like unintelligible waves, but no one said a word to her. Only smiles were exchanged, a silent celebration of the imperfection and limited power of the technology and an indication of the growing sense of collective alienation to the entire event. The active enactment of backstage, it seemed, was a means not only for redefining group boundaries, but also for resisting the technological means that imperil its social space.

By the time Liz's words became intelligible again, members engaged in various activities: drawing tiny pictures on pieces of paper, bouncing a small rubber ball on the table, gossiping, exchanging all sorts of unrelated organizational information, silently going out to get coffee. Each of them was displaying partial mental detachment from the formal conversation that was now freely flowing through the speakerphone. Each was exposing to the group a portion of self that was concealed from the eyes of the participants from New York. Moreover, in the whispered Hebrew discussions and pantomime conversations, these concealed portions of self often displayed a variety of attitudes that were shorn of social posturing: boredom, anger, cynicism, impatience, indifference, annoyance, or other seemingly authentic manifestations of the "real" selves of people who, in the confines of backstage, appeared to feel at home.

Moving on to the next item on the agenda, Barbara from New York asked if Ori, an engineer, was present. "I am here," he said, verbally declaring his presence to the distant others. "You've asked me for a switch," Barbara said, "are you really using this for the system?" Ori explained at some length why the switch was indeed needed, and when he finished talking the speakerphone was silent. "Barbara?" he asked. Muteness persisted. Merav tried to help, explaining that, "We are switching because of capacity problems." Barbara finally responded, "Our question is different," but Ori insisted, "We are even considering another switch," and Udi elaborated: "Barbara, hi, this is Udi speaking. Just now we are in the midst of testing." Barbara uttered "Mmm. . . . Right," and then, while trying to say something, she burst into a giggle. Some other amused sighs and unsuccessfully held-back laughs were heard through the phone. It became apparent then that the active construction of a bounded backstage amidst this boundary-crossing event was not exclusive to the local side. The participants exchanged gestures of puzzlement, and someone whispered in Hebrew, "They are laughing." Unable to determine what exactly was implied by the outburst, members were obviously taken aback. Still, their collectiveness hardly seemed disturbed by this recognition. On the contrary, their reciprocal gestures implied that they were experiencing emotions together. Refusing to lose face, however, Udi continued talking as if nothing had happened. He alone was sustaining the formal definition of the situation until both backstages were hidden again. Soon enough, the conversation was back on track.

When the participants moved on to the second issue on the agenda, a senior manager from the Asia-Pacific Marketing Department, Dori, walked into the room. In the organization's jargon, this department was one of the team's "internal clients," and Dori came to represent its interests with regard to certain issues that were listed on the agenda. Dori, it should be noted, was hierarchically senior to all of the conference call's participants except Eytan, who was his equal. He sat down quietly. Preferring to stay in the backstage, he did not announce his presence to the participants from New York for quite a while after his arrival, and the conversation continued without his direct participation in it until the Asia-Pacific Department was brought up. When he did join the conversation, his demands stirred an argument that warrants close scrutiny because it cut through the enacted backstage boundary.

The argument concerned a project-training event that the team had to organize. Bill and Mark from New York said that the Asia-Pacific's training would be combined with another event while Dori requested several days of separate training for the department. Supporting Dori, Eytan said: "Mark, I really recommend that it take place on a separate day. This is how we did it here before. We declared a certain day for training and everyone cleared that day specifically for that purpose. Is that acceptable for New York?" Yet Dori did not want a separate day but separate *days,* and added: "Eytan, let me modify a bit what you're saying. The Asia-Pacific Department is very scattered. I think that while it would not be justified to fly people from all over the world to the training, it would be justified to ask you to give several separate training sessions within the region." Merav shook her head. "I am not sure that I agree with Dori," she declared, crossing the local boundary by joining the other side of the argument. "In fact, we had some trouble before with such a separate training in . . . mmm. . . ." Seeking help from her surrounding locals, she looked up and asked in Hebrew, "what is the name of our office in the United States?" Dori answered "Albany," and she continued, "Right, our office in Albany." "Furthermore," she said, looking at him, "you know that we can only do it at the end of April." Dori replied: "That is far too late!" Merav insisted, "But it takes time to prepare it . . ." and then, suddenly retreating into backstage, she said, "it takes *zman* (the Hebrew word for time)." She continued her argument with Dori in Hebrew: "Look, this is what Gadi (the EVP of Product Marketing) said." Dori silently shook his head in disagreement, signaling not only his refusal to the training plan but also, through the silence, to conducting the argument while "on the air." Understanding this, Merav told the New York participants that she would take it upon herself to conduct further inquiries, wrote down an "action item," and requested to move on to the next item on the agenda. The argument was suppressed, drawn from front-stage, but its significance cannot be overlooked: the image of a harmonious, undifferentiated "we" had cracked under the pressure of role interests.

Once the argument subsided, however, boundaries were quickly reconstructed. Shortly after the change in the item of agenda, the participants from New York declared a time-out because they had to move to another room. While they were offline, the locals talked about them. They discussed "the Americans'" political position in the organization: "They won't do anything because they are so scared of R&D over there"; agreed on the fact that "We have to get them moving already"; and even designed a strategy for confronting the problem: "Tziki should simply go there with the platform and say to them: 'Here I am, now let's check the platform already!'" Thus, in a sense, they were jointly plotting a scheme of control, claiming command and status by asserting the organizational interest as their own, and posing themselves as belonging to the supposedly better or more responsible side. "Eytan?" an annoyed voice asked, putting an end to their discussion, "Thank you for the Hebrew lesson." Aware of the sarcasm, the entire group immediately grew silent. "Oh, I am sorry . . ." Eytan said, apologizing for all of them. "I thought you were still offline."

After some further discussion, Dori, the senior manager, rose. He asked for a small rubber ball that lay on the table, threw it to Tziki, and they playfully started shooting it into a small basket hanging from the wall. The ball was flying above Merav's head. Pretending to point a gun against Dori, as if getting ready to shoot him, she whispered, "Stop it!" He sat down for a while, but then apparently got bored again, got up, walked over to the desk of the EVP of Product Marketing, and glanced at the photos of his smiling sons. Suddenly, he called out: "What do you say, Mark—maybe we should do the client demo in their Beijing facilities?" His look was one of amusement, as if he was playing with the New York participants, waiting to see how they would react to a provocative remark. Barbara's voice sounded anxious as she said, "Let's see if I understand what you are saying. You are talking about the demo? About the demo, right?" Dori smiled: "Exactly."

Merav whispered to Tziki, "Isn't it obvious that he's talking about the demo?" Mark started answering, but the connection was disturbed again and his words were obscured. Dori waited some time until he finally said, "I think we have a line without echo." New York's participants hung up and dialed again, and Barbara continued talking about the demo. Dori smiled at Merav and Tziki, whispering, "She said this once already." Approaching the table, he pressed the mute button and said, "Are you seeing what they are saying? They want us to be their de-buggers!" The participants grinned and nodded in agreement. Dori's behavior—his stroll around the room, his basketball playing, his amused attitude, his mocking behavior, his declaration about what "they" want from "us"—seemed to convey to those present that he was now relaxing the boundaries of his managerial identity (the boundaries that separated him from practically all of the conference-call's participants, including those sitting in the room) in order to join the local collective; to "act out" a local affiliation. Indeed, since he *was* a senior manager, his taking such an active part in the backstage dynamics seemed to endorse them with a seal of legitimate authority. Playing it manager with some—namely, the Americans—and playing it pal with others—the locals—Dori turned formal authority itself into a boundary-setting device.

More than an hour had passed since the beginning of the conference call, and, as the discussion continued, the local participants were growing increasingly restless. Two of the engineers, Ori and Udi, left. When Eytan explained something technical to the members from New York, Merav asked Alex in a loud enough Hebrew whisper that the manager in Paris could hear, "Is this true?" Heard online, her question incorporated Eytan in the backstage dynamics at the price of making them evident to the team members from New York. Alex gestured with his hand that he had no idea if what Eytan was saying was true, and Merav said, "I don't think it is true either, but it convinced them." Everyone smiled. Merav pointed at her watch and said, "Come on, it is really getting late, let's get this over with." The call was now at its final stage, and the group was jointly awaiting its termination. As if cooperating with them, the connection suddenly collapsed again, and Merav said in Hebrew: "Oh, this is just the time to end this." In English she said, "We're losing you again." But the connection was again recovered, and Barbara asked Tziki another question. His impatience growing increasingly obvious, Alex asked in Hebrew: "What is she talking about?" and Merav answered, "She is just babbling now." Eytan, in Paris, asked in English, "I have one more question, is Ori still there?" "No," Merav answered, "he left a loooong time ago!" "Okay then," Eytan replied, "I think we've covered all the issues." "Bye-bye"s were exchanged. Someone's finger touched a button, and the final curtain descended. The sense of a distinct, Hebrew-speaking collective, socially sustained throughout most of the call, withstood the technological, structural, and social challenges that were posed against its defining boundary and even seemed to be reinforced by them.

Virtual Politics: An Email Exchange

Ami is a technician who worked in one of the Customer Support functional groups. Before the merger, the group—a small and specialized unit—reported to a senior Customer Support manager who was unfamiliar with its professional work. Accordingly, the group's members enjoyed considerable autonomy. However, after the merger the group was additionally subordinated (through a matrix structure) to Jake, the manager of a parallel group in New York who was more familiar with its activities. This change in the reporting structure may seem minor to an outside observer, but was in fact very significant to the people involved. It gave rise to various political dramas, one of which began on a Friday morning when Kelly, one of Jake's American subordinates, sent Ami and two members from the Israeli Customer Support Department (as cc's) the following email:

From: Lewis, Kelly
Sent: Friday, March 6, 1998 10:43 AM
To: Ronel, Ami
Cc: Cohen, Alon; Ramon, Omer
Subject: X2 and X3

Ami, Alon, Omer-
I was planning to send over the new X2 and X3 designs to you today but after having a conversation with Jake, he would like them to follow the original X1 format. The reasoning that he is using is that we may soon be embarking upon a new design and it would just add to the confusion in the interim to introduce something else. Our product is already getting a bit too confusing.

So, they are going to be re-laid out in the original format and this will take another day or so. I hope to have them to you on Tuesday. I will be traveling abroad and will be out of the office most of Monday and Tuesday. I still need to get edits on X3, but we will just lay it out with what we have and make the copy edits later.

I hope this will be okay with you. If so, we can have the X2 and X3 printed within 7 days after getting final approval on the new files I will be sending over.

Regards,
Kelly

Kelly sent this email on Friday, a day that for most Israelis is a day off from work. Her message awaited Ami on the net until Sunday, the first day of the Israeli workweek. Answering the email, Ami addressed his response not only to Kelly, but also to Jake the manager and to three locals (as cc's): the two internal clients from Customer Support and the group's original manager:

From: Ronel, Ami
Sent: Sunday, March 8, 1998 6:23 PM
To: Lewis, Kelly; Smith, Jake
Cc: Mor, Kobi; Cohen, Alon; Ramon, Omer
Subject: RE: X2 and X3
Importance: High

Kelly, Jake, Hi!
One of the messages to come out of our meeting in Tel Aviv with Jake was that the current X1 design is being phased out, and a new one is about to be introduced. This met with agreement from all sides.

To base the new X2 and X3 on the obsolete design not only sounds extremely unclever, it goes against agreed policy.

I strenuously object, and advise the Customer Support managers not to accept this either.

Ami

Email writers enjoy power that is based upon their ability to select their audience, and Ami's response is a case in point. Utilizing global technology to challenge the global organizational structure that granted authority to Jake, he grouped together a chosen audience to witness how he greeted Kelly before Jake, spoke as Jake's equal, and openly challenged the manager's professional expertise. In other words, he chose an audience to witness a political drama that asserted his own professional authority and autonomy. Furthermore, the audience was not only witnessing this textually created drama but also heightening it. Ami was showing his local organizational clients—the cc's—that it was he rather than the new manager from New York who was continuing to act in their best interest, showing Kelly his public attack against their joint manager, and showing Jake that he was able and willing to show all this to all these people. Technologically monitored inclusion of an audience thus constructed a practical arena for Ami within *and* through which he attempted to assert his power over the superior from New York.

Kelly's response to this letter arrived on Monday morning. In an email marked "confidential" she wrote Ami the following message:

From: Lewis, Kelly
Sent: Monday, March 9, 1998 6:55 PM
To: Ronel, Ami
Subject: RE: X2 and X3
Sensitivity: Confidential

Ami-

You'd never even know you had an agreement in Tel Aviv! I told Jake I was working on the new designs and he told me that these should look like the old ones. I tried to tell him that was not what we had talked about and not what you were going to be satisfied with, but he didn't care. I hope you realize that I am merely the messenger on many of these items. His direction, or serious lack of, is the real culprit. It is causing confusion and problems in many other areas . . . not just the designs. It will be interesting to see him work on a project while I am gone.

Need to run to catch my ride to the airport. I would like to talk with you on Wednesday if you have some time. I am very, very frustrated, Ami. I almost feel embarrassed by some of the things I am being asked to do . . . they don't make sense! I just can't help feeling that this lack of direction can't go on much longer . . .

Kelly

Reacting to Ami's public charge against their joint manager, Kelly thus forged an explicit bond with him. She marked a new circle of identity, and its boundaries separated the two subordinates from their manager. These boundaries were enacted through the exclusion of Jake, and within their confines Kelly revealed an inner, emotionally "true" self that detached itself from the links that tied it to the joint manager. The Isrocom-Amerotech boundary had thus been relaxed, and a managerial-subordinate boundary was delineated instead.

As a response, Ami wrote two different emails, one to a local audience and one to Kelly. These emails are an example of boundary-management; of an attempt to favorably monitor the intersection of a local and global identity (that of being an Isrocom member and that of being a co-subordinate) in a way that is politically rewarding. In the first email, Ami addressed the group's original local manager and another Customer Support manager (as cc). Note that Kelly's previous email was attached to it:

From:	Ronel, Ami
Sent:	Tuesday, March 10, 1998 10:27 AM
To:	Mor, Kobi
Cc:	Shiran, Doron
Subject:	This situation cannot continue!
Importance:	High
Sensitivity:	Confidential!

Kobi, Doron, Hi!

The exchange below is self-explanatory. It looks like we are about to lose the only good person we have in New York.

I do not intend to continue investing in an already awkward and burdensome working relationship with them if Kelly leaves.

Please do not further embarrass Kelly by disclosing to anyone in New York that I forwarded this to you.

Ami

It is interesting that Kelly was very much *in* this email: her email was attached to it and she was repeatedly mentioned. Nonetheless, she was not included as a recipient, and since her confidential email was attached without her knowledge, it turned into a device of her own exclusion. The content of Ami's email broadened this effect: it construed Kelly as a resource that a local "we" might lose; as a stark symbol of the inferior worth of the merger partners ("the only good person" in an otherwise "awkward and burdensome working relationship"); and as a rationale for the exclusion of "anyone from New York" from the organizational flow of information. Kelly's attempt to forge a shared identity with Ami was thus redefined and used to mark out Ami's shared identity with a group that she helped define but did not belong to. In this sense, her boundary-blurring move was ironically used to bolster the boundary.

Exclusion, however, was incomplete. Eight minutes after he sent the first email, Ami sent a second email that was addressed to Kelly alone. It consisted of a partial depiction of the email that she was excluded from:

From:	Ronel, Ami
Sent:	Tuesday, March 10, 1998 10:35 AM
To:	Lewis, Kelly
Subject:	RE: X2 and X3
Importance:	High
Sensitivity:	Confidential

Kelly, Hi!

Wow! You seem to be at the end of your tether! I'm so sorry that I have to be a part of that process. I apologize for some of the arrows that I have hurled in your direction—you were not the target. I know you are only the messenger. I appreciate your work and your talent. As a result of your email below, I have let Kobi and Doron know that I think you are the only good thing in New York, and without you I do not intend to invest in the already problematic working relationship between Tel Aviv and New York.

I look forward to talking to you tomorrow.

Fondest Regards,
Ami

Thus, in this email, Ami reaffirmed his bond with and commitment to Kelly. Again, however, as in his previous email, he expressed his boundary-crossing commitment in a way that actually reaffirmed the boundary: reporting to Kelly, after the fact, that he had presented her to local managers as an exception to a problematic organization, he emphasized his membership in a local collective while isolating Kelly from hers, and assertively declared the burden of otherwise crossing the line "between Tel Aviv and New York."

In sum, by selectively expressing his attachments to his local others, on one hand, and to his remote peer, Kelly, on the other hand, Ami navigated between his social ties. Sustaining the local-organizational identity, the "us"—expressing his membership in and commitment to it—but also sustaining a global sense of affiliation to an American co-subordinate, he turned both into a political resource that he directed against the "problematic working relationships" with New York. The global technology of the email offered him the ability to easily manage inclusion and exclusion and thus to reconstruct and manipulate the same social boundaries that it also helped to overcome.

Discussion

The two technologically mediated communication events were characterized by boundary-setting processes. In both, technology narrowed down communication channels, turning all that was seen and whispered (in the telephone case), or all that was written to a confined, carefully selected audience (in the email case) into a "natural" backstage; an easily sealed-off social terrain within and through which members could enact a locally bounded sense of belonging. Dori, Merav, the engineers and the others who participated in the conference call and also Ami in his email message to the local others displayed unity and cohesion by speaking as an "us" facing a burdensome or problematic "them," as well as by suspending occupational, hierarchical, departmental, or other distinctions amongst themselves. Furthermore, they revealed a "true," seemingly authentic self to the local-organizational others who participated with them in the communication events: a self who spoke Hebrew (a taken-for-granted if not automatic linguistic choice, but nevertheless carrying the symbolic overtones that sharing a mother-tongue can convey), or felt at home, or displayed real, uncensored attitudes toward those who, regardless of overall, formal definitions of unity, remained "the Americans," "them," or "New York."

Thus, while the organization may have been formally defined as global, in these communication events members generally preserved the local boundary that once separated them from Amerotech's members despite the work processes and goals that now bonded them together. They engaged in a social and symbolic effort to designate this original local boundary as well as to display their attachment to those who were on their side of it. Technologically mediated communication events, then, became a practical arena in and through which members expressed and manifested a locally circumscribed sense of organizational affiliation.

However, members' social and symbolic efforts were incomplete. They left room for two types of challenges. First, processes of construction did not go so far as to completely repudiate the large, global "we"; the overarching and united identity that encloses both merger sides. For one thing, in both communication events an actual dialogue did take place, information did flow, and work was coordinated. Furthermore, at times it seemed that what the locals were trying to do was not to undermine the global as much as to monopolize it; to claim the global territory exclusively to themselves. In the scheme of control that the conference call participants plotted and in Ami's emails, the locals talked as the knowledgeable representatives of the global organization's interests and goals, depicting their merger partners as slow, lazy, or burdensome. "We know very well," writes Laclau (1995: 99–100), "that the relations between groups are constituted as relations of power—that is, that each group is not only different from the others but constitutes in many cases such difference on the basis of the exclusion and subordination of other groups." Indeed, in Isrocom, too, members' symbolic effort was not only one of excluding but also one of subordinating, or delegitimizing, the merger partners. The combination of these two elements had a paradoxical effect: members rejected the global definition of unity only to claim superiority in embodying the global organization's ideals. The locals, in other words, rejected the idea of "Globalint" in one sense, but strongly embraced it in another.

The second challenge to the re-enacted local organizational boundary was the expression of other identities that cut through it. For example, both Merav's occupational siding with her American colleagues in the argument that evolved during the conference call and Ami's structurally forged affiliation with Kelly as a co-subordinate in the email exchange undermined any notion of a clearly delineated local boundary. These global attachments, in other words, challenged the assumption of a boundary that separates every member of the "us" from every member of the "them." Indeed, they were monitored accordingly: Merav abruptly withdrew the argument from frontstage and Ami sought to rhetorically isolate Kelly ("the only good thing in New York"). In both events, in short, the challenge of a global affiliation surfaced and was monitored so as to minimally interfere with the boundary-setting process.

Indeed, global technology, too, helped monitor the surfacing of these global attachments. The mute button, for example, allowed the participants in the conference call to adjust the formation of these global relationships and offered possibilities for selective performances: for being one thing to those there and another to those here. In the email exchange, the addressee selection option, as well as the delayed nature of a semi-"live" drama, offered Ami the possibility to manipulate boundaries of identity to his advantage. Global technology thus offered possibilities not only to easily sustain a backstage but also to tightly control the front-stage. The next subsection will deal with cases in which these boundary-monitoring possibilities were not available.

Face-to-Face Communication Events

Face-to-face communication events between the merger partners were relatively rare. They involved expensive and time-consuming travel, and thus necessitated solid justifications in order to be approved and carried through. Usually, only a small number of visitors would arrive, reducing the costs of travel to a minimum. Such face-to-face gatherings were also scheduled well in advance in order to ensure the efficient use of the visitors' limited time, and formally predesigned to accomplish specific organizational purposes. The two most common types were training events and meetings. This section offers accounts of each and then concludes with a comparative discussion that analyzes the main findings.

Turning Away from the American Way: A Training Event

It was a beautiful spring morning, and around thirty Israelis, most of them project managers from the Asia Pacific and EMEA (Europe, Middle East, Africa) marketing departments, were gathered in the lecture room of a luxurious Tel Aviv hotel. They came for a sales training on Amerotech's product. The lecturers were two project managers from New York, Tim and Bart.

The first lecture was to begin in about five minutes. In the meantime, the participants were strolling around a buffet table, stirring coffee in little cups, tasting pastries, and engaging in small talk. During this time, I talked with the lecturers Tim and Bart, and with two participants, Yonatan and Shira. "The merger was a blow for me," Bart said, "I understood the business rationale, but emotionally it was very difficult. I'd been working for Amerotech for five years, and suddenly they changed the name, the logo. It's been very dramatic for me. There is a change in the atmosphere, people are leaving the company . . ." Nodding in agreement, Yonatan responded with a description of the difficulties that he endured as a consequence of the merger. "It hasn't been working out," he said, "it just hasn't been working out! We agree on things and then it takes us a month to discover that they didn't understand what we agreed upon, that things are not getting done." Both Bart and Yonatan thus presented themselves as belonging to distinct sides, but now that Bart's difficulties had been matched, they were also bonded together through common experiences of merger-hardships. This seemed to make way for a more personal tone in the conversation. Yonatan was asked about his excellent English, and he explained: "I am not really an Israeli, I am originally Australian, but I've been living in Israel for twenty years." "Do you feel more Israeli or more Australian?" Bart inquired, and Yonatan answered: "Actually I am a misfit both here and there, but I am less of a misfit here." "I guess that I am too, I am from Nicaragua," said Bart, delineating a common identity as immigrants. Shira, a multi-language speaker, said some words in Spanish, and they laughed. The original topic of conversation revolving around merger experiences of members of two distinct organizational belongings underwent somewhat of an unexpected turn. It shifted, within seconds, to Israeli and American, Australian and Nicaraguan, and, finally, immigrant and native identities, redrawing boundaries and making them permeable, assembling attachments in search of a commonality.

However, the transition to the more formal parts of the event entailed a gradual denial of commonality. The first boundary that was publicly managed, albeit with some unexpected consequences, was that which set apart the audience from their lecturers. When it was time to begin a lecture titled "Configuration," Tim and Bart walked up to the front of the room, opened a slides-folder on their laptop computer, lit the projector, and a large chart with tiny and crowded characters flashed onto the large white screen. With their cups of coffee and pastries in hand, the participants sat down. "The number on the seventh row is wrong," a senior EMEA manager named Nadav joked about the crowded chart, humorously undermining the lecturers' status while, at the same time, acknowledging it by taking a seat. Adding to his joke, Shira referred to the title of the chart, a made-up company called "Hear Me Out Company," and said, "Is this a Chinese company?" Nadav grinned, and pronounced the title with an imitated Chinese accent: "Himi-ot . . ." Members of the audience laughed. Bart laughed, too. Yet Tim, quite clearly of Chinese descent, did not seem amused. The joke—a friendly ice-breaker? a stark display of bad manners and insensitivity?—momentarily rearranged identity boundaries, marking new bonds and borders by the distribution of laughter and anger in the room.

Then the lecture began. Tim projected configuration charts onto the screen and discussed them. The participants asked technical questions that were predominantly based on comparisons of configuration tools. Clearly, however, there was more to their questions than technical curiosity. Used to working with a different set of sales tools, the participants seemed to listen to the lecture from the standpoint of a group that was committed to its own ways of doing things, and these comparisons were at least in part contests over worth. For example:

Ran: "Let's say you need to add these blue colored configuration items, can you do that?"

Tim: "Bart and I are not experts on this."

Ran: "No, because our spreadsheet does have it. I am not saying, hey hey, we got it, but . . ."

Nadav (the senior EMEA manager): "Maybe we should talk about creating a possibility to cut and paste more blue items onto the sheet."

Tim: "My answer is that it is just a matter of adjustment of the spreadsheet."

Ilan (another senior manager): "I want to add a comment. (Stands up, turns his back to Tim and faces the audience.) Those of you who are from Asia Pacific, bring these cases to me. We need to take action items on these odd applications."

Thus, the technical discussion became an occasion for members of the audience—superiors along with subordinates, those from EMEA along with those from Asia Pacific—to delineate a local "us" by referring to its distinct work methods, and to assert its superior value. Tim was outnumbered as well as overpowered by a crowd that included senior managers. He continued to deliver information, demonstrating a cut-and-paste procedure on the laptop computer and growing laconic and apparently distant in the face of his audience's questions. When the demonstration was over and Nadav, demanding the final say, declared that the spreadsheet was too automatic, Tim did not reply. A loud, uncomfortable silence filled the room until finally Bart caved in. "It is too simplistic," he said, giving the audience what it wanted. With this the lecture ended.

But the conflict did not. In Tim's next lecture, "Pricing," disagreement resurfaced and tensions heightened. After several slides were shown, one of the participants asked a question concerning pricing calculations. When Tim answered, Nadav the senior manager turned to a subordinate who sat behind him, and told him in Hebrew, "He simply does not understand pricing." His words—told to one but apparently directed to all—were heard across the room, linguistically excluding the guest lecturers and molding members into a single, managerially endorsed, Hebrew-speaking side. Ignoring the Hebrew comment as well as the murmurs that accompanied it, Tim explained that in New York a special pricing team was responsible for the task of calculations. "They are the experts on this issue," he said. Nadav asked in return, "Are you saying that every quotation has to go through them?" "Yes," Tim answered, "and they can help you." Saar, Nadav's subordinate, raised his hand to ask another question, but Nadav told him in Hebrew, "He doesn't . . . he just doesn't understand." Turning to Tim, Nadav asked: "Is this information available only for people from Finance? It isn't available for project managers?" Tim replied: "No, I am saying that they can help you." Loud whispers in Hebrew followed this statement, and Tim and Bart looked at their audience in puzzlement. Finally, Saar explained: "*We* are the project managers and *we* do pricing." An occupational identity common to the lecturers and their audience was thus registered as an arena of strife between them. Tim's reply was, "Yes, but the structure is different. Part of our role here is to expose you to the structure in New York and how it works." Clearly growing impatient, Nadav referred to the new joint intranet and asked: "Does the pricing sheet exist on the net?" Sigal, a participant who happened to be in charge of the local Marketing intranet site, called out: "No! This is exactly what I talked with Bart about: having it sent to me."

The reference to the intranet spurred a number of related questions that were directed to Sigal, and it looked as if the lecturer had lost control over the proceedings. The local participants were no longer joking, no longer comparing: by now they were blatantly hostile. They were actively seeking a way to bypass and exclude the pricing experts from Amerotech and, in effect, bypassing and excluding the lecturers standing before them. Nadav's lead had thus been followed, and his exclusionary talk became action. Seeking to regain control, Tim finally projected three slides in a row. The first read "Tactical Pricing: A Team You Can Count On," and the second and third consisted of smiling pictures of the pricing team's two members, Derek and Tina. Trying to protect them from the sudden revolt that undermined their utility, Tim turned to the seemingly universal rhetoric of work virtue and said: "They are the pricing experts. They are in the loop. They are very quick and they have experience and expertise. They reply within half a day. They sometimes work on weekends." Several participants, including Nadav, demonstratively walked out. A participant named Yoram said, "I want to request that the spreadsheets will be available on the intranet so that I will not have to turn to them for it." Tim answered: "I would discourage that. They are the experts and they are very quick." The gap seemed unbridgeable, and once again it was Bart who acted as a mediator. "I suggest that you nonetheless write it down as notes," he told Tim. "What I am seeing here is . . ." Someone from the audience interrupted him and called out: "Cultural difference." Rephrasing with more technical and perhaps less loaded and polarizing terms, Bart replied: "There is a lack of fit between current procedure and requested procedure." Rina, a participant sitting next to me, whispered to me, "Do you realize what is going on here?" "What?" I whispered back. Rina said:

> The people here are used to doing this themselves, every one of us does it on his own, and Tim just continues to market the two pricing experts from New York. He should have ended this presentation by now, it is ridiculous. Bart is the smarter of the two, he realized this, but Tim is just going on and on.

Note how Rina rephrased Bart's rephrasing, once again defining the gap that was exposed in local terms, as one existing between "what every one of us does" and what exists in New York. While commending Bart, she rejected his attempt to use more neutral, bureaucratic terms to define the situation ("a lack of fit between current procedure and requested procedure"), complimenting him instead on the effort to somehow sum up Tim's "ridiculous" presentation.

Ending his lecture, Tim repeated: "I encourage you to call them." A participant named Gur referred to the two pricing experts and asked his colleagues in Hebrew, "Did these two try to do pricing for Net (Isrocom's product)?" Tim somehow figured out what Gur asked, and answered, "It's up in the air. The pricing system is very different." Gur looked at him, obviously taken aback: throughout the event Hebrew had served as a powerful means of exclusion, and yet by answering the Hebrew question Tim demonstrated that linguistic boundaries are hardly airtight. Apart from information that tone and timing can convey, the Hebrew language is thoroughly riddled with English names and terms, especially when technical matters (such as Net) are discussed. Apparently, much could be understood even by a foreigner. Closing the technical lecture with this social lesson, Tim turned off his laptop and gathered his papers from the desk. Gur turned to Ilan, his manager, and only half jokingly said in Hebrew, "Let's get a hold of this Tina, let's let her do our pricing for us. I like the idea—a team like that." Though Tim was at least to some degree linguistically and socially excluded, the idea that he had presented nonetheless flowed through the lecture despite the conflict that evolved. Gur admitted this in Hebrew and only to another local. Furthermore, he apparently balanced the admission with what seemed to be a touch of machoism in his reference to Tina, conjuring up gender boundaries in place of the local boundaries that he had crossed. Ilan, however, refused to play along. "She won't do pricing," he said, "she will do analysis." One of Gur's colleagues, Amir, added that "She may know how to write from left to right,[2] but any little thing that you will ask her to do, anything just a bit unusual—she won't know how to do it. Just forget about it." Local boundaries were thus reaffirmed, and Gur was impelled to obey them. "In short," he conformed and even surpassed Ilan's and Amir's generalizations, "she'll do it the American way."

Battles and Drills: A Meeting

During one of the crisis periods in the Gulf, close to the expiration date of one of the ultimatums, at a time in which many Israelis stood in line for gas masks, preparing themselves to face one of Saddam Hussein's threats, a group of members from New York arrived for a series of meetings in the Operations department. Their hosts bought them gas masks, just in case, but they didn't tell them so until they arrived. "I thought of asking them to bring gas masks with them," the manager who organized the meetings told me, "because the lines here are very long. But we decided not to bring this up. They are adults, they have enough people to turn to over there if they don't want to come, and we decided that as long as they don't bring it up, we won't bring it up." The locals, it turns out, made a conscious effort to silence a situation that defined their location as dangerous and disadvantaged. Their silence, like their guests' silence, blurred or obscured boundaries, but only in the most superficial way. Not only was "the situation" un-silence-able—it was broadcast on practically every news channel and printed on the front page of all major newspapers— but their effort marked them out as a separate group with joint interests, a joint scheme, and a shared (silent) social face.

The meetings were designed to exchange updated information as a means for facilitating the integration of work processes and coordinating activities between the two shop floors. I waited for the first meeting to begin near the open-space cubicle of the department's secretary, Yona. The Vice President of Operations, Zohar, had not arrived yet, but his subordinate AVPs from Amerotech and Isrocom, Nick and Shlomo, had. There was some uneasiness in their waiting until finally they started talking about Yona's computer. She was away on an errand, so Nick sat in her chair, Shlomo stood behind him, and they both looked at the screen and discussed the computer's programs and capabilities. Global technology is a universal topic of discussion; an international icebreaker. When Yona returned, Nick said to her half jokingly, half apologetically, "You left and we took over. You've got to be careful!" The "we" that he spoke of consisted of two senior male managers who shared status and authority that apparently allowed them to invade the physical and cyber space of a secretary. With the formal meeting not yet begun, they had found the common ground upon which to manage their co-presence.

The expression of commonality, however, was soon challenged. Shlomo asked Yona about a work matter and, acknowledging the presence of an American guest, he spoke in heavy accented English that seemed somewhat unnatural in a conversation between two Israelis. Yona answered him in Hebrew. "You have to speak in English because Nick is here," Shlomo told her, paying his dues to his colleague but also demonstrating the effort that the foreigner's presence entailed for him and Yona as Israelis; illustrating how the national boundary between them weighs down on his own demand, deeming it "unnatural" if not wholly implausible. "Oh, it's okay, it's okay," Nick excused them, politely consenting to his own exclusion. Yona laughed an uncomfortable laugh, turned to Shlomo, and they completed the conversation in Hebrew.

Time passed and Zohar, the VP of Operations, did not arrive. Finally, Shlomo ushered Nick, a subordinate named Gili who had also arrived to take part in the meeting, and myself into the meeting room. "I think we will start as soon as Zohar gets here," he said, acting as the temporary man in charge. After everyone was seated, he went outside to check what was going on with the VP, met him in the hallway, and came back to announce that the meeting could begin because Zohar would not be joining it after all. Following this announcement, he took the absent VP's role throughout the entire meeting: he was the one to introduce everyone, to declare transitions from one item on the agenda to the next, and to ask questions in an authoritative, demanding tone. Despite the fact that he and Nick were of identical formal status, it was he, the local, who became the manager of the situation; an authoritative host to a foreign guest.

The meeting began with a presentation that Nick had prepared and that concerned the ways that shipment issues were dealt with in Amerotech. Projecting the first slide of his presentation, a shipping plan with Globalint's logo on top, Nick told his small audience, "You're probably already familiar with this format." Shlomo replied, "You're working with this data, you don't have to apologize for it." Nick, evidently surprised by the insinuation, was quick to retaliate. Now that his presentation was reframed as explicit admittance of lesser value, he undertook a counteroffensive by saying: "It is probably difficult for someone who sees it for the first time to understand." "No," Shlomo answered, his voice cool and collected, "these are just configurations."

After this skirmish things calmed down for a while. As if allowed too evident an expression, the competitive hostility was jointly suspended. Nick projected more slides, his presentation flowed on, and the discussion that ensued seemed professional. Presenting Amerotech's methods and comparing them to those of Isrocom, the lecture did focus on boundaries and contrasts, and yet, temporarily, it seemed to highlight a commonality: the fact that beneath it all was also a joint occupational language and understanding. Indeed, even though significant work differences were presented, and even though there were obvious differences in the participants' accents and demeanor, habits and routines, it nonetheless seemed clear that they also shared the same basic occupational mindset and terminology.

So, for a while the "Shipment" presentation sailed calm waters. Soon, however, hostility resumed. "Excuse me," Gili (Shlomo's subordinate) said, interrupting one of Nick's explanations, "where do you calculate the margin?" "Mike has the data," Nick referred to an economic analyst from Amerotech's Finance department, "he does it." Pressing his point, Gili referred to a certain item on the slide, and asked, "Then what is this for?" Nick sighed. "That's really a financial call." Shlomo shook his head. Joining his subordinate's line of questioning and thus making it evident that they were of one opinion—jointly critical toward the delegation of responsibility and authority to someone from outside the department—he added, "That's also Mike's responsibility?" "Right," Nick answered laconically, his expression indicating that he was well aware of the sting. Then—refusing to further delve into the issue—he immediately put up a new slide titled "Production Forecasts."

The discussion was by now openly hostile. "These are the latest numbers?" Shlomo asked after several slides were projected, clearly dissatisfied with what were apparently below-expectation forecasts. Nick seemed uncomfortable: rumors had it that Amerotech's shop floor would eventually close down (see Chapter 2), and the question of the economic justification of its existence was thus of crucial significance. Taking out another slide, he said, "I'm not asking for your sympathy, I just want you to understand how it works." Placing the slide on the projector, he sarcastically uttered, "I understand that there is no sympathy here." Ignoring his remark, Shlomo turned to Gili. Slipping into Hebrew, they discussed the numbers in a hushed tone, agreeing that some data is missing from the slides. Nick watched them in silence. Finally, Gili got up and left the room, explaining that he was going to bring the local "Forecast and Order Management Form" to show him. Guessing what the two had talked about before Gili left, Nick told Shlomo, "Most folks, I am sure the skeptics in Tel Aviv, will probably doubt that we are going to make it." The boundary that delineated his "we" from "the skeptics in Tel Aviv" thus engulfed the future as well: organizational fates have not been merged, regardless of formal rhetoric. His guess concerning the topic of the hushed, Hebrew discussion was on target and Shlomo answered, "Well, you rely upon a job order that is a big question mark." Then, as Gili walked in with the form and handed it to Nick, Shlomo pointed at items that did not appear on Nick's slides, and asked, "So when are you going to ask your suppliers about *these* items?" "Oh, I don't ask them . . . our poor suppliers . . ." Nick said, "they're like in a drill until June . . ." "Because of the merger?" Shlomo sounded amused, expressing further detachment from Nick's "our suppliers" and implicitly landing what seemed like another hostile blow: as far as formal requirements were concerned, suppliers, like clients, were not to be sympathized with but rather reassured that, despite the merger, it was "business as usual"; that for them nothing had changed. Nick's empathetic phrasing, "poor suppliers," was hardly in accord with the formal public relations effort, and Shlomo's comment seemed directed at that unwittingly admitted disparity (while, in fact, also manifesting it: he spoke in the name of the global merger only as a means for further provoking the tensions that sliced through it). "No, no," Nick said, sounding apologetic. "We just told them that they will reap the fruits of their labor a little later. Jane went there to talk to them and . . ." Obviously not interested, Shlomo impatiently interrupted him and declared that he would like to discuss another matter. Nick shut off the projector. His presentation was over.

Discussion

The training event and the meeting were marked by processes similar to those observed in technologically mediated communication events. In both of these face-to-face engagements, members displayed their commitment to a local and distinct organizational entity, in part by arguing for the superiority of its ways. Suspending distinctions that cut through this local side, namely those between departments or between managers and subordinates, members enacted a unified "front" and defended the status of local processes and methods. Moreover, their active cooperation was also registered through acts of exclusion that became strikingly evident in these scenes. Since face-to-face events lacked the "natural" backstage that emerged through the use of communications technology, all that was seen—back turns, facial expressions, hushed Hebrew talk—made exclusion not only blatant and highly perceivable, but also, as Nick's bitter utterance ("there is no sympathy here") indicates, somewhat cruel to those who were cast aside by it. In this kind of engagement, in other words, the distinct and separate organizational identity was played out very much "in the face" of the merger partners, without the relief of the technological curtain.

Nevertheless, despite this fact, here too the local-organizational identity project was to some extent partial. Most crucially, there were ways in which members embraced the idea of globalization after all. Thus the training event and the meeting *did* take place; information did flow between members who endorsed—willingly or not, by their mere co-presence—the idea of joint membership in a single organization. Moreover, the overt contests over value that evolved in both engagements—which spreadsheet is more efficient, which pricing procedure more effective, which data more precise, which production forecast more realistic—endorsed rather than undermined the united, global organization by turning its goals and ideals into a basis for comparison and a criterion of value. Carried out in support of rather than against the global "good"—indeed in the name of the merged organization's interests—these contests over value reaffirmed the notion of "Globalint" even as they rejected the definition of unity that it implies.

Moreover, the local identity project was challenged in other ways as well. There was, for example, that "Himi-ot" joke that rearranged boundaries, a flow of meaning about pricing that transgressed them, Bart's attempts to mediate and find compromises, and Tim's and Nick's proven ability to partly overcome linguistic exclusion. Furthermore, there were also occasions in which various identities that cut across the enacted boundary rose to the surface: that of immigrants in the training, male managers in the meeting, and occupational colleagues on both occasions. These identities seemed to overshadow, at least momentarily, the local-organizational "us" that was enacted, undermining its homogenous surface with a sense of divergent, boundary-slicing, global commonalities.

And yet it was, indeed, momentarily. While meaningful, the challenge of global commonalities was, on the whole, peripheral, socially curtailed as Guy's remark about Tina in the training or overshadowed by strife. On the whole, it seems plausible to say that the dominant process in the face-to-face scenes was one of setting local boundaries, not crossing or overcoming them. Enacted "in the face" of the merger partners, hostility was unleashed to counter the effect of co-presence, for once space and time converged, all that was left to mark the "realness" of the boundary was the vigor of members' own insistence.

Conclusions

During communication events members of Isrocom made a concerted effort to enact a bounded and distinct organizational identity. As illustrated in the four scenes, this effort was full of spontaneous twists and turns, unexpected spins, and ambiguous consequences that originated from the intricate fabric of everyday life. However, analytically speaking, it generally consisted of two major elements. First, members often took part in acts of exclusion. They acknowledged the presence—real or virtual—of merger partners but, at the same time, rejected their status as interaction partners. They defined social boundaries by restricting part of the social dynamics to local participants. In technologically mediated communication events this restriction was upheld by the technology itself, by the fact that it offered the possibility to "mute" communication channels and thus create an easily sustainable backstage. Nonetheless, there were other resources of social restriction, most prominently Hebrew, and in face-to-face communication events these were used in a more visibly clear way, constituting what seemed to be a more extreme version of social exclusion. On the whole, in both kinds of communication events, engagements with the merger partners became both the arena of and the means for expressing disengagement from them.

The second element was asserting unity and congruity amongst the locals. Just as the Isrocom/Amerotech boundary was enacted through exclusion, the boundaries that separated Isrocom's members from each other were suspended through locally undifferentiated *in*clusion: regardless of internal distinctions, those who happened to participate in the communication events enacted themselves as "one." This oneness had both verbal and behavioral manifestations. Verbally, participants often spoke of themselves in plural, glossing over internal distinctions with the utterances "us" or "we" and with repeated references to things "ours": our work methods, our place, our structure. Inner variety was thus masked by the verbal convergence of collective selves and collective possessions. In the four scenes that were depicted, such rhetoric was usually complemented by behavioral displays in which internal distinctions were downplayed. Thus, for example, in the conference call the engineers and the product managers suspended their occupational distinctions; in the training event members of the two marketing departments suspended their structural distinctions; and on various occasions, managers—namely, Dori in the conference call, Nadav in the training event, and Shlomo in the meeting—suspended their hierarchically differentiated, managerial identity in order to engage in boundary-setting efforts with their subordinates. During communication events, in short, members acted in a way that helped sustain a local, collective "public face" (Cohen 1986: 13) that fused together internal differences.

The collective "public face" of Isrocom's members seemed to give a socially concrete form to a separate and locally defined notion of organizational membership. Engaging with the merger partners, members displayed their exclusive attachment to those of the pre-merger Isrocom. They turned all that was designed to attach them to the merger partners—common product planning, data sheets, pricing procedures, marketing missions, production forecasts, and so forth—into a means for demarcating themselves from them. In the global communication events members thus expressed a distinct organizational identity, a sequel of the independent Isrocom identity, and in a way its "purest" manifestation: an internally inspired expression of belonging to an organizational collective, lacking any apparent or concurrent form of formal inducement or pressure.

This account does not coincide with the prevalent view in the organizational literature. Most strikingly, in contrast with the tendency of many organizational theorists to assume the exclusive power of the formal system to define the organizational identity, here it was members who enacted the boundaries of their organizational "us" as well as what it means to belong to and be a part of it. It was they who, in the midst of everyday work-life, acted as the purveyors of a local version of organizational membership despite the global definition of unity that was imposed upon them by the very act of a merger. If anything, the power of the formal system was itself subordinated to this task, reappropriated by those to whom it was delegated—managers—and used by them to endorse the local effort. Specifically, as managers such as Dori (in the conference call) and Nadav (in the training event) tended to maintain a biased display of their formal power, to disregard it with some (locals) and manifest it with others (merger partners), their official status was symbolically recruited to the local identity project. The formal power of the global system, in this sense, had turned against itself.

The persistently manifested local-organizational identity also seemed to recruit the national identity to its purposes. Basically, the "us" and "the Americans" who were spoken of were at the same time organizational and national. By thus tightly coupling these identities in single expressions, members fed into the definition of the merger situation the assumption that a nationally predetermined, preexisting boundary outweighs the formal definition of unity. They conjured up the national identity in a way that helped reconstitute the boundaries of the local-organizational identity.[3] At the same time, they also seemed to elicit some new meanings with regard to this collectively reconstituted organizational "us." Consider, for example, the repeated instances of Hebrew talk during the conference call. Such instances appeared to invoke among the Hebrew-speakers a collective sense of "realness" and authenticity, togetherness and commonality, symbolically endorsing local boundaries not only through the obvious exclusion of the merger partners but also through the sense of domestic ease that sharing a mother-tongue can convey. The overlay of organizational and national affiliation thus also infused the former with a meaningful symbolic overtone.

Accordingly, while it is plausible to assume that many of the processes that were observed in the communication events would be prevalent in any organization undergoing a merger, there seems to be something unique about the fact of a cross-national merger. In such a context, members have an especially powerful and compelling symbolic resource with which to both convey boundaries and express communality: their national identity (Ailon-Souday & Kunda 2003). Indeed, as it increasingly becomes the central and standard terminology for issues of identity (Ben-Ari 1996), the symbolic resource of national identity is not only powerful but also highly available. In Robertson's terms (1992: 135), it constitutes an accessible part of globalization's "general mode of discourse about the world as a whole *and* its variety." Thus, in contrast to the cross-cultural view, which stresses national cognitive gaps—those disparate mental softwares that are imbued in people's minds (Hofstede, 1980)—the findings here seem to point to national identity's potent and widespread *symbolic* role in attempts to construct a sense of difference rather than to its psychological role in generating a so-called fact of difference.

The repeated expression of a distinct and separate local-organizational identity nonetheless left room for counter-processes. While sealed-off through exclusion, homogeneously glossed over through verbal and behavioral inclusion, and anchored in preexisting national boundaries and meaning, this identity was also challenged in various ways. Most critically, the formal version of a merged, global organizational unity was never completely rent asunder. Alongside the continual boundary-setting processes, the communication events also indicate that information continued to flow between the two sites, as did a considerable degree of cooperation. Furthermore, they indicate that membership itself and the legitimacy or value of the organization's globalness were never seriously questioned and were even used by members to claim to their local "us" a privileged normative position. There was, in short, some manner in which the "them" were, after all, a part of the "us."

In addition, engagements with Amerotech's members also entailed the surfacing of non-organizational global identities and related flows of meaning that cut through any reconstructed sense of boundary. A variety of such identities surfaced in the scenes that were described, for example "we" the subordinates, "we" the marketing engineers, "we" the immigrants, "we" the men. It is true that members usually withdrew their boundary-breaching commitments just as quickly as they were expressed, silencing them, overcoming them, pushing them to the periphery of social interaction. But even the shortest and shallowest expressions of such commitments seemed a potent reminder that every person was more than a member of the single, local organizational "us," and hence a potential transgressor of the boundary that defined it. Engagements with Amerotech's members, in sum, brought to the fore not only the constituting experience and validation of difference between the locals and their merger partners, but also the challenge of emergent commonalities.

It thus appears that when the formal and structural bases of a social boundary are blurred, the struggle to redefine it becomes a struggle over the boundaries of self. The multiplicity of identities that exists for each person seems to pose a constant challenge to the overall effort of sustaining a single identity for the (local) collective. In a sense, taking part in the process of social construction demands of people to choose a self out of what postmodernists like to call their "decentered" selves: out of their pool of potential identities. It demands that they navigate between various affiliations that rise to the social fore. Agency, in this sense, is not only external, expressed through social behavior, but also internal, for there are no automatic choices, no mutual-exclusiveness of identities as theorists of organizational globalization tend to assume.

And yet, while the local-organizational "we" did not automatically cancel other, crosscutting senses of "we," it did seem to set the impetus and underlying rule for navigating between them. The fact that the identities that Isrocom's members shared with their merger partners were repeatedly silenced, overcome, or pushed to the periphery of social interactions indicates something about the power of the local, collective identity-project to restrain multiplicity and fragmentation. The postmodernist notion of the "decentered self" should in this sense be balanced with an acknowledgement of the social dynamics that tame it. Ideas about fluidity and undecidedness should be countered by theoretical awareness of the capacity and force of the social situation to at least partly center the decentered self.[4]

It is with regard to these issues of "navigating" and "centering" that the most crucial significance of global technology seems to lie. Within Isrocom, global technology did not appear to globalize identities as much as to offer a means for selective, biased performances; for ensuring that the surfacing of a global, boundary-blurring affiliation would be monitored so as not to interfere with the efforts to maintain the local-organizational one. Moreover, as illustrated through Ami's exchange, the email offered possibilities not only to monitor emergent commonalities with the merger partners, but also to manipulate them to one's advantage. In other words, global technology offered means for a flexible navigation between social ties and for the manipulation of the social world. Thus, in the case of Isrocom's merger, members did not use information-technology to solidify virtual, global ties as much as to give them over to the concrete, local ones.

In sum, during communication events with merger partners from Amerotech, Isrocom's members made a joint effort to sustain a distinct, separate organizational identity. This effort involved, on one hand, maintaining a local boundary through acts of exclusion and through the symbolic recruitment of national identity. On the other hand, it involved asserting insiders' unity. While ongoing, this effort never went so far as to completely repudiate the formal, global version of an organizational identity and even reaffirmed and sanctioned it. Moreover, physical and technologically mediated co-presence also held the potential for the surfacing of various crosscutting, nonorganizational identities and related schemes of meaning that turned members into transgressors of the same boundary and the same internal sense of unity that they concertedly sought to sustain. Continually tackling these challenges, members used the information technology to create a bounded and controllable "backstage," or resorted to explicit hostility as a means for acting out boundaries face-to-face. While unable to overcome the constant potential of rupture, they sustained the local-organizational identity project in a way that was vigorous and pervasive enough to be deemed a dominant aspect of the communications events that were described.

Communication events were, however, limited in terms of their time span. Much of organizational life played itself out in the absence of the merger partners. What happened when "the Americans" were neither physically nor technologically present? How did members refer to them whilst engaging amongst themselves? How were identities enacted in interactions that were confined to locals? It is to these questions that we now turn.

CHAPTER 4

Identity and Representation

Placing the Merger Partners on Display

"Look around," Asaf, one of the so-called "victims" of the merger bitterly told me several days before he left the company, "the Americans are everywhere." Though perhaps a biased observation springing from an angry and frustrated point of view, his remark nevertheless did contain some valid truth. In a way, the merger did turn "the Americans" into an inseparable part of Isrocom. Symbolically represented through talk, photographic displays, and written texts, they were continually discussed, looked upon, referred to; continually called up in the mind. In this sense, their presence did indeed extend beyond communication events to Asaf's seemingly unlimited "everywhere," and they became an integral part of the local "here and now" even in their absence.

The importance of studying such representations concerns more than the fact that they were, in this sense, "everywhere." Generally, representations play a critical role in processes of identity construction (for example, King 1997; Hall 1990; 1997). Transcending the actual presence of the others depicted, they inspire a continual sense of difference that lingers on far beyond and often with no direct relation to immediate, intergroup encounters. Furthermore, representations do not only inspire a continual sense of intergroup difference, but also, in effect, constitute it. Characterized by the tendency to impose accentuated and coherent imageries upon the always broken and intricate rubric of experience (Hall 1990), the act of representing is often one of encoding "otherness" into the others who are depicted (Hall 1997; 1997b), and, by the same token, forging congruity upon identity and what it means to belong (for example, Hamilton 1997). Representations, in this sense, offer not only a perpetuating documentation of the "them" but also a means with which to constitute the "us" and imbue it with meaning.

This chapter focuses on such representations. It explores the notions of organizational identity that were constituted through depictions of Amerotech's members within Isrocom. In what follows, I present detailed descriptions and interpretations of relevant events in which verbal, visual, and written representations were put on display and members reviewed and responded to them.

Verbal Representations: Talking Identity

The most routine way of representing the merger partners in the local site was that of talk. As they became an integral part of everyday life, members of Amerotech were often mentioned or referred to in ongoing discussions and conversations among locals. While taking endless forms and shapes, most of the talk may be categorized into three major types in correspondence to the physical context in which it typically unfolded. The first type was hallway-talk: spontaneous and usually friendly conversations among acquaintances who happened to run into or informally approach each other. The second type, meeting-room talk, may generally be described as formal, work-related, and usually hierarchically mediated conversations designed for reports and coordination. The third kind of talk was assembly-room talk. Rigidly structured, it consisted of speeches performed on special occasions by senior managers. The next three scenes are examples of each. They are followed by a comparative discussion.

Moshe's Tricks: Hallway Talk

Yuval, a middle manager working in IT, reported to a senior American manager. When I interviewed him, I asked if I could attend one of his group's weekly conference calls. Yuval didn't know when the next call was scheduled to take place. He escorted me to the office of Moshe, a colleague who also reported to the same manager, introduced me, and told him about my request. Moshe said that these conference calls were always scheduled for Monday at four p.m. "Yes, but this Monday we have to go to Ofer's father's funeral," Yuval reminded him, defining a "we" by the imparity of involvement in the private and local life of a particular employee. "There is also a problem with Monday the following week," he added. Moshe nodded in agreement. "Is this Monday afternoon a sacred thing?" Yuval asked, demonstrating through the question itself how *unsacred* and burdensome the cooperation arrangement was for him. "I really don't like it." "No, no," said Moshe, "I think that we can probably change it." We agreed that I would call Moshe in a day or two, after he'd have a chance to contact the boss from New York.

Yuval and I left the office and walked into the hallway. "You know," he told me, "Moshe and his subordinate Seffi were abroad last week, and they managed to pass a decision that the ERP system would be centered here. When they left it had already been decided that it would be centered in New York, but they managed to alter the decision. It is going to be here. This proves that not everything in this merger is about honor-games—sometimes logic prevails." Moshe overheard Yuval's remark and came out after us. "It isn't logic!" he cried, and, as we turned around to face him, smilingly added: "If you'd have heard the tricks we had to play over there in order to bring the system here!" Moshe had thus admittedly acted on behalf of a common local interest and now, as he stood smiling before us, he was apparently demanding recognition for it. His demand marked him, Seffi, Moshe, and even myself as members of a distinct collective not only because of the territorial interest that we presumably shared as locals, but also because we were now in on a scheme that was designed against members from New York. As he turned to walk away, he added a finishing touch to our enacted status as his accomplices, teasingly saying what we now jointly perceived as a part of his "tricks": "No, no . . . there is logic in it, there is logic. . . ."

Thus, Yuval's positively framed depiction of an underlying logic shared by Isrocom's and Amerotech's members—his talk of a possible commonality that transcends the "honor games" between the merger partners—was reinterpreted by Moshe, his colleague. Demanding social recognition, Moshe molded the representation of the reported event in a way that reconstituted the notion of two competing sides, imposing this polarity upon Yuval and myself by implicitly including us within it. We, in turn, did not resist this representation but merely said our own goodbyes immediately after he turned away, passively endorsing the reasserted assumption of two distinct sides, if only by not contradicting it.

Pizza, Coke, and the Politics of Difference: Meeting-Room Talk

Natan's R&D group was established after the merger. It consisted of software engineers who had extensive experience with Net, and who were responsible for developing its interface with Amerotech's product. Like every other R&D group in Isrocom, the group held a review meeting every several weeks to discuss the status of the projects under development.

This project review, like many others, was held in a small, windowless meeting room on one of the R&D floors. More precisely, this was not a room but a redecorated war-shelter:[1] the dangers of Israeli locality do not skip over any building, even if it is inhabited by an enterprise as global as Globalint. As the first several members came in, the seats around the table were quickly taken, and people wandered off to search for chairs in adjacent rooms, carrying them back in and placing them against the walls. By the time the meeting began, the room was packed full of participants who were crowded in the narrow space between the table and the walls. The group's secretary then came in with a surprise treat: trays of pizza and bottles of Coke. It was almost lunchtime, and members thankfully greeted her as she entered. She put the food down on the table, and then left the room. The pizza trays were passed around, handed from one to the other. In the middle of all this, quite unexpectedly, the room was filled with the sound of water being flushed in a bathroom behind the walls. There was a loud silence and then a burst of laughter, and it seemed to redefine the unwelcomed intimacy with the anonymous person from behind the walls and turn it into a jointly constructed intimacy with the people within them. It was crowded in the room, and the concerted expression of gratitude to the secretary, the mutual pizza offerings, the collective eating, and the joint management of an awkward event filled the room with an atmosphere of cozy togetherness. This meeting constituted one key occasion on which I came to appreciate the social significance that sharing a space can convey.

"Ido," Natan said, turning to one of the team leaders, "let's start with you." With a slice of pizza in hand, Ido began listing the status of projects that were currently being developed by various members of his team. When he referred to a project that demanded exceptionally precise coordination with engineers from Amerotech, Natan interrupted him. "You've just returned from New York," he said. "Do they understand the same thing that we do or don't they?" This yes-or-no question constructed a singular "they," an enunciated totality of place and mindset that was somehow equivalent to and perhaps validated by the oneness experienced in the room. By the way it was phrased, the question pressed Ido to generalize the organizational others he had met and bind them as a unit in one single representation. Ido, however, was apparently having difficulty living up to this tacit expectation. Describing the complexity that was involved in his contacts with members from Amerotech, he emphasized the fact that processes of understanding defied simple "us" and "they" categories, and said: "As a result of the reviews that were held between August and now, there were changes in the (project's) interface. In the beginning it did fit the product in New York, and then there was an upgrade. It took us two review meetings to understand it but finally we agreed that . . ." Impatiently cutting him off, Natan repeated his question more harshly, making it clear that he was interested in plain results and that the in-between details of the process were a nuisance to him. "To what degree are you *certain*," he authoritatively said, "that we are doing the same thing that they are doing?" Thus, Natan spoke in terms of our understanding and their understanding, our doing and their doing, insisting that the major issue of significance—the core constituent of the situation—was a gap between two sides. "After the review with the subcontractor," Ido said, "it looks like they are talking about the same thing." Making up for his only partially concealed uncertainty, and further framing "the same thing" as something that demands special effort and focus on his part, he added: "But I am planning to travel to New York during the integration phase and I will make certain that we're all talking about the same thing . . ." Thus, facing a managerially sanctioned impatience for detail, Ido yielded to Natan's construction of the situation in the sense of committing himself to action that was based upon it, while, at the same time, still registering a potential "we're all" that to some extent challenged it.

But Ido's was not the last word, and even the future potential of "we're all" was soon challenged. Among the participants in the review was a project manager who did not belong to the group but who was responsible for a certain client with an interest in Ido's project. He joined the conversation between Ido and Natan and commented that the client requested a tight development schedule that would fit its own business needs, posing it as a prerequisite for further investment. "Were there consequent revisions in time schedules?" Natan asked Ido and then added: "Because in your interactions with the Americans you are not only supposed to make sure that the system works, but also to make sure that any possible trouble with deadlines is avoided." Following and exceeding Natan's lead by suggesting the complete exclusion of "the Americans," another team leader joined in and said, "Aren't there any product applications here, so that we can check everything here, without them?" "No," Ido answered, "New York's applications assume a bandwidth that we don't have here." Natan summarized the discussion by saying, "Please enforce the schedules in the interaction. Include them in the plan." Ido nodded in agreement and wrote his superior's request down. He had come a long way in one short review: at first insisting upon a unitary, global representation, he ended up agreeing to monitor a side consisting of "the Americans" who were likely to think and do different things and who might create trouble with deadlines.

Toast!: Assembly-Room Talk

On the last day of work before the Jewish New Year, the members of the Production Group from the Operations Department were invited to attend a toast for the holiday in the new spacious and elegant dining room that had recently been opened on the fifth floor. A while had passed since the last meal had been served, and the dining room was now clean and empty, with a tiny bouquet of fresh flowers on every table and a well-known Israeli pop song playing in the background.

Toward the intended time, members started to flow into the dining room, and it grew increasingly noisy. "Hello everyone," Yossi, the manager of the local production group, called out, silencing his subordinates' conversations.

"We have to begin and not wait for the last arrivers because we have a client visit, and this is the most important thing for us." He waited a while, letting his clear priorities sink in, and then began a short holiday speech:

> We are now gathered in the new dining room. Those of you who had a chance to visit the old dining room on the fourth floor have to admit: it is amazing how we ever managed ourselves in the old dining room. You must appreciate the new!

Speaking as a "we," Yossi thus presented the local gathering place, namely Isrocom's new dining room, as a concrete expression of impressive growth and success. Strengthening this imagery, he then offered another concrete, local example, this time from the production group itself:

> And if we are mentioning territories, then I would like to tell you that when we moved into this building we planned Net's production areas in (—) million dollars, and we thought that it would be enough to bear the load for a very long time. But the production areas will already be fully operational by the end of next year. This means that we have to prepare ourselves. It takes time to plan and implement new production areas.

Note how Yossi's "we" was uniformly deployed to describe what were, in fact, distinct social units, thus rhetorically blurring differentiations that cut through the local collective. Specifically, while the "we" who "moved into this building" generally represented all those who were present, the "we" who "are mentioning territories" blurred the distinction between the speaker and his audience, and the "we" who "planned Net's production areas," "thought that it would be enough to bear the load," and "have to prepare," blurred the distinction between management (such information was usually reserved for management circles) and workers. Through this boundary-blurring "we," Yossi masked inner distinctions with a single, unified representation of a successful, locally experienced collective. The audience, for its part, was by now completely silent, all eyes focused on the speaker. They seemed almost a cohesive 'one,' endorsing with their attention his rhetorical effort.

Continuing in the same vein, the manager further aggrandized the organizational accomplishment by mentioning the skeptics lurking on the outside:

> I didn't mean to give a long speech but since the beginning of the year, since the beginning of the merger era, there has been continuous production and growth despite the market's and the analysts' doubts. They inspected us with a magnifying glass and we did not let them down. Globalint reached (—) million dollars of sales.

After mentioning the joint, overarching organizational identity, "Globalint," and exalting it with a mention of its acclaimed achievements, Yossi made a small, albeit crucial reference to its two merged parts: he made a distinction between the contribution of the two organizations to success—

> Within Globalint, Net's contribution was more than two-thirds and the contribution of New York's product was a third.

Thus, Yossi utilized the common—"Globalint"—to construct a notion of two parts within it, as well as of his own part's superiority. In other words, in this section of his speech Yossi outlined the commonality at the basis of difference (Barth 1969) and grabbed its "shared vocabulary" (Ben-Ari 1996) to his side's advantage. Consequently, he invoked the local site not only as a jointly experienced symbol of global success, but also as its principal constituent. Note also, that as he compared the relative contributions of Isrocom's and Amerotech's products to Globalint's success, he laced together the discourse of identity with the discourse of capitalist management, infusing the local-organizational "we"—the side that ostensibly made the larger contribution—with overtones of capitalist pride and self-worth. This paved the way for specifying future goals for the production group with the implicit expectation that the greater status of the local "we" would be obligating in terms of the future contribution of its members:

> These proportions will not change dramatically. Perhaps the opposite is true, perhaps the proportions will grow in favor of Net. If we add to this growth our other goals and the demand of the Customer Support Department that we will assist them with the upgrade and with that which is designated to replace the product platform by next year, then we have very high targets ahead of us.

The sense of a distinct side, of a bounded identity, was thus conjured up to spark motivation; to serve the attainment of the production group's goals. Further strengthening this effect, the manager ended the speech with compliments on goals that had been accomplished by "the Israeli Operations" during the passing year:

> But we are on the right track. We set ten goals for this year. We examined the progress this week and found out that at least with regard to Net's share, at least with regard to everything that is related to the Israeli Operations, some of the goals have been accomplished by the middle of the year. Costs reduction, for example: I was happy to find out that the plan that I presented to reduce costs was accomplished already. This is a very nice performance. And I don't want to underestimate other goals that all of you took part in their achievement. This is the holiday season and it offers an opportunity for the workers and their families to rest. I want to wish us all a happy holiday and a happy new year, and I wish that we will all refill our batteries because we need them!

By stirring emotions of belonging and participation, Yossi constructed an imperative to actively contribute to the production group as a means for enhancing the status of the local collectivity. Countervailing the global identity claim put forth by the very notion of Globalint, he inspired his subordinates to make a local identity claim of their own through high performance and achievements. This rhetorical effort, it should be noted, was immersed with paradox: managerially designed to spark workers' motivation, Yossi's "we"-talk could not override the fact of a managerial act of power. In other words, the speech was itself a blatant symbol of the same internal distinctions that it rhetorically denied.

Now that it was over, Yossi and his assistants hurriedly left the dining room to meet the important client. A member who sat next to me asked his friend, "This is it? It is over?" His friend answered, "Yes." Cynically referring to the lack of refreshments in this New Year toast event, the latter pointed to the small flower vase that decorated the table and added, "Here, drink this water as a toast!" The holiday event was thus redefined, used to express the subordinates' protest rather than overall cohesion. Yossi's attempt to endorse a local "us," to stir up and sustain a sense of a mobilized, cohesive collective, could not override and thus lived in tension with division and friction from within.

Discussion

The three scenes have several characteristics in common. To begin with, in each of them the possibility of global bonds with the merger partners was voiced: Yuval's talk about a common, underlying ERP logic, Ido's depiction of a shared process of understanding with Amerotech's engineers, and Yossi's mention of Globalint in the New Year's toast event. Since the Americans were absent, the possibility of global oneness had to be voiced in order to be contradicted, and, indeed, in each of the scenes this possibility was eventually abandoned. The final word was that of those who sought to reimpose a scheme of locally defined difference upon their listeners: Moshe the IT team leader who asked for recognition, Natan the R&D manager who demanded compliance and relief from detail, and Yossi the product group manager who sought to inspire motivation. Each of them, it seems, bolstered the local boundary by molding representations of merger partners in accordance with their own interests or needs. Members from Amerotech were thus depicted as having a disparate goal, a discrete agenda, or dissimilar achievements in relation to those of the locals.

But while having the final word, the polarized representations voiced by Moshe, Natan, and Yossi seemed to be somehow counterbalanced by the apparent passivity or reservations of their listeners. Yuval and myself in the hallway, Ido in the meeting room, and the production workers in the dining room appeared to be willing to listen and cooperate, but not in a way that expressed homogeneity and unity from within. On the contrary, internal social and hierarchical differentiations proliferated in the scenes that were described. As was perhaps most evidently illustrated in the cynical flower-vase remark in the New Year toast event, the listeners in these scenes eventually reacted in ways that registered a fragmented inner quality, one that did not coalesce into a simple symbolic statement matching the representation of the American others. Accordingly, despite the fact that they were framed in terms of common, collective interests tied to the local place or local product, Moshe, Natan, and Yossi's attempts to re-establish a sense of boundary through representations of the merger partners' otherness were implicitly challenged in that they could not overrule the flavor of a discursive act of power; of doubt concerning the role of particularist interests in their enactment (a colleagues' interest in gaining social recognition, a manager's interest in securing compliance, and a senior executive's interest in inspiring motivation). Indeed, as was illustrated in the second and third scenes, which focused on formal events—a professional meeting and a holiday toast—the flavor of a discursive act of power was at times rooted in authoritative power. The managers used the authority granted to them by the global organization in a way that helped constitute a sense of local boundedness within it.

Taken together, these verbal representations thus marked the simultaneous strengthening and loosening of the local-organizational identity that was enacted during communication events of the sort depicted in the previous chapter. On one hand, the local "we-ness" was strengthened because the merger partners' absence gave some members freedom in fashioning dichotomous representations in accordance with their own interests; in strategically imposing images of a split. On the other hand, it was loosened because the reactions to these representations were only partially cooperative, marking segmentation with regard to the inner quality of the local collective. Verbal representations thus marked a complex tradeoff between depictions and reactions. The next subsection will examine this tradeoff with regard to the second major kind of representations that were observed in Isrocom: visual representations.

Visual Representations: Seeing Identity

Displayed images of the merger partners consisted of managerially sponsored photographs of them. There were two major kinds of such photographs in Isrocom, each of them displayed in a different way. First, photographs documenting joint, face-to-face communication events between members of

Isrocom and Amerotech hung for display on walls. Second, personal photographs of workers were displayed on the intranet system. This section presents two scenes, each concerning a different kind of photographic display. The two scenes are followed by a comparative discussion.

The Kosher Lobster: Photographs of a Joint Event

Every department in Isrocom had its own bulletin board. Usually, it hung on a wall that was adjacent to the open-space cubicle of the department's secretary. After an organizationally sponsored social event such as a departmental vacation trip or a holiday party, the usual content of these bulletin boards was often replaced by a variety of snapshots from these occasions, displaying smiling faces of members eating, hiking, dancing, resting, or swimming together. This was always a radiant and cheerful assertion of a collective, harmonious face; a happy "us" smiling down from the walls and displaying to every worker a "me" that was content and joyful in the presence of the department's others.

In a similar vein, after a group of marketing managers returned from a joint event in New York, their department's bulletin board was filled with photographs from this occasion. Three groups of photographs were crowded together on the board. First, there were photographs that displayed a volleyball game from a variety of angles. Members were informally dressed in T-shirts and shorts and organized in mixed teams. They were throwing the ball, watching it fly above the net, falling on the ground in an attempt to hit it, raising their hands in a sign of victory. Apart from the background scenery of a wide lawn and a dark forest, which is very different from the familiar Israeli scenery, this looked very much like all the other fun-event snapshots commonly displayed on bulletin boards. A joyous "us" decorated the corridor: a single fun-filled whole consisting of smiling, similar-looking figures that manifest in their photographed moments of concerted play an idealized, unified version of a global collective and that defy any suspicion of slicing local-boundaries.

The second group of photographs complemented the first. It consisted of snapshots taken within what seemed to be a typical hotel conference room. Each picture displayed a different member giving a lecture to the colleagues. They were talking business now, not playing, but the photographed images seemed just as much those of a unified and harmonious collective as those of the playful occasion. Not only did the audience look like a single and homogenous group, but the series of speakers looked very much alike: each stood in the same spot, wore a business outfit, and had a similar expression. These photographs did not display heavy Hebrew accents, different styles of lectures, or the occasional remark or hushed whisper that were probably heard in the audience. Rather, they depicted a polished collective; an aesthetically harmonized version of the social reality of this particular management team.

While I was examining this second group of pictures, a member of the department, Shimon, walked by. Just as he turned to enter his office, he teasingly said to me, "Did you see Rafi (the department head) eating a lobster?" This turned my attention to the third group of photographs. They were taken in a restaurant, and, in resemblance to the other two groups of photographs, they displayed smiling members happily engaged in a lobster feast. These members were photographed wearing large aprons on their chests with pictures of red lobsters drawn in the middle, their mouths full or smiling at the camera, holding a mug of beer up in the air or pointing down at lobster-filled plates. Once again, they seemed like a happy, unified, homogenous group. Yet Shimon's remark reframed this image and turned it into a partial and shallow depiction. He turned my attention to a picture of Rafi, the department head, eating a lobster, because Rafi is a religious Jew[2] and lobsters are not kosher: eating them is forbidden by the religion. Moreover, lobsters seem to be among the most prominent symbols of people turning away from the Jewish religion and choosing to lead nonobservant if not completely atheist lives. Accordingly, the photograph of Rafi sitting at the table with a skullcap upon his head and a lobster-apron tied around his neck, holding a mug of beer in one hand, a red lobster in the other, and opening his mouth toward it as if ready to take a bite, was, to put it mildly, a striking image.

I stood there for a long while, staring at the picture in disbelief, both convinced by what I saw and trying to figure out what I was missing. When another member named Rotem walked by, I pointed at the photo and asked: "Did Rafi really eat a lobster?" "No," she replied, laughing at my gullibility. Still confused, I nodded in puzzlement and she explained: "He was holding a plastic lobster." "Did you eat a lobster?" I wanted to know. "Are you kidding," she said, "we had a feast!" The social world was thus comfortably reordered: the nonobservant dined, the observant did not. Rafi, to be sure, did go far: in order to hold even a plastic lobster and take part in such a lobster feast he no doubt had to compromise much as it was; to sacrifice something of himself for the sake of the image of unity. However, he could not control how his resultant image would be read—a sign of strength? a sign of weakness?—nor could he prevent the plastic lobster from symbolically "backfiring" and turning his photo into a parody of sorts: a ridiculed pretense that demonstrates not the crossing of boundaries but their persistence and strength. After all, as his subordinates well knew, Rafi didn't really eat a lobster. Thus, while neither Shimon, Rotem, or myself are observant Jews, the mentioning of Rafi's personal religiousness seemed to undermine the collective, unified, harmonious representation of the international management team by bringing to mind not the sameness it shows, but the divisions it so superficially hides. Glancing again at the entire display, the pointed-out parody seemed to have had a spillover effect: in the shadow of Shimon's smile, the management team appeared to represent an organizational reality that was as distant from a "true" global option as a plastic lobster is from a real one.

Image Games: Personal Photographs on the Intranet

The joint intranet system that was put to use during the initial stages of the merger contained an alphabetically ordered members' list. Each member on the list had a separate web page that contained both general information about her or him—name, role, department, email, telephone numbers—and a smiling photo of the kind usually displayed on passports and identity cards. When one scrolled through the list continually, these pictures would flash on the screen one after the other, face after face, smile after smile. Furthermore, there was also the possibility to search the list by specific keys: to select from the pool of images and details those that depicted specific people. This was the way members usually looked for telephone numbers or email addresses. Furthermore, if they happened to work with a person they had never met before, the search option also offered a certain relief from curiosity: at the touch of a button the image of that person would flash on the screen, offering a face that one could think of as her/his interaction partner.

Symbolically, the list seemed to imply "personalization" in the sense that, as a representation, it detached members from any sign of subgroup attachments. More specifically, the list was characterized by the representational absence of any sign of sectional belonging. Each individual was displayed on a separate page, each page had an identical format, and the aggregation of pages was ordered in a neutral, alphabetical way. By thus manifesting separateness, homogeneity, and neutrality, the list as a whole depicted an undifferentiated organizational collective; a mere aggregate of individuals.

Members often described this address list as the most popular site on the intranet. At times, however, its utilization was not directly work-related. Absentmindedly flipping through the images, some would engage in a playlike activity of trying to guess whether the smiling snapshots belonged to Americans or Israelis. Then they would check the names to see if they were correct. This game was played either individually or in couples, and as Tomer, an engineer, told me, "Most of the times our guess is right." National identities, it appears, could somehow be read from the images despite the similarity in the form of the snapshots. The process of identifying national origin was thus rendered a fun, internally motivated activity, one that invalidated the joint, neutrally organized list of images by exposing the underlying, nationally defined boundaries it covered up.

There were, nevertheless, other variations to this game. Sometimes identity games cut through the local side. For example, Orna, a worker from Operations, would search for the snapshot of her manager to view (and show) how funny he looks in it. Uri, an engineer, once illustrated to me how image flipping is for him also a way to examine women. "The main utility of this list," he explained, "is for single guys. We gossip: did you catch a look at this one or that one, and then we search for the photograph and take a look." Image flipping was thus an identity game that concerned identifying different kinds of different Others. While at times used in a way that marked off national identities, it was also used to enact other identities that sliced through the local side, such as those related to hierarchy or gender.

Discussion

Visual displays of the merger partners were organizationally sponsored representations that had been molded in a way that emphasized harmony, unity, or similarity. In the team photographs that were taken at a joint event and in the intranet list of personal photographs, members of the "them" were represented as an integral and undifferentiated part of the "us." These photos were thus self-consciously assembled depictions of a global option.³ As far as reactions were concerned, these harmonious and unified images encountered resistant responses. Challenging them, members rendered the global depiction a partial or problematic representation by playfully pointing out variations in the identities of the people whose images were displayed: the parodied religious identity of Rafi, for example, or the game-invoked national, hierarchical, and gender identities of some from the intranet list. Members, in other words, contested the managerially sponsored, visual global displays with counter-representations of variance.

As far as the local-organizational identity project was concerned, these resistant representations were to a large extent counterproductive. By registering identity variations, members challenged not only the assumption of oneness among members of the merged entity—of the united Globalint—but also of oneness among members of Isrocom. Thus, Shimon's mentioning of Rafi's religious identity undermined the harmonious image of a cheerfully unified global management team by bringing to focus the differentiations it conceals. His remark had complex consequences: on one hand, Rafi's photo demonstrated the possibility of playful reconciliations, of identity-compromises. On the other hand, the photo also demonstrated the limitation of such compromises, touching upon a deep divide that splinters the local collectivity no less than the global one. Similarly, the same kind of image games that undermined the unity and homogeneity of the global list of photographs on the intranet also undermined any sense of the congruity and oneness among the locals, marking out genderial and hierarchical boundaries that cut through the local side. Resistance to unified depictions of a global collective thus undermined the constructed assumption of the commonality of the local collective, pointing out its own internal fragmentation.

Textual Representation: Reading Identity

As they became a part of the global work processes, Amerotech's members were repeatedly referred to in internal organizational documents. These documents included, for example, email messages such as those described in the previous chapter or reports used mainly for documentation such as meeting summaries and project progress reviews. During my stay in Isrocom I attended one event in which a very central and important organizational text—one that members read constantly and continually in the course of their work—was discussed: an intranet training event. This event offers an opportunity to examine not only a textual depiction but also members' reaction to it.

Surfing the Organizational Cyber Space: An Intranet Training

As mentioned earlier, the intranet was Globalint's internal information network. Originally a merger-dowry from Amerotech, it was implemented in Isrocom during the initial weeks of the merger. The task of adding to it information related to the local site took a bit longer. In terms of its design, the intranet was quite similar to the regular internet. Its main page listed three main kinds of information pools. On the top left corner was a list of general intranet sites (such as Home, Address Book, and Search). Below this general list was a longer list of all the organizational units, offering links to information organized according to departments and divisions. The rest of the main page consisted of information pools grouped by content, each represented by a large icon: for example, a cup of coffee for "Daily Essentials," an open book for "Document Service," four people holding hands for "Employee Services." A double click on any item in the lists or on any one of the internationally readable icons offered access to related intranet pages. These contained either actual information or more specific lists and categories of information to choose from as one "surfs" the joint pool of corporate data and knowledge.

Once most of the information related to the local site was processed into the network, Miri, one of those in charge of implementing the system, began a series of intranet training sessions. I attended one such training session at the end of May. With me at the training were about a dozen members from the EMEA marketing department.

Projecting intranet pages from a laptop computer to a screen that hung in a large, oval conference room, Miri began with a review of the general list. She double-clicked the "Address Book," explaining to participants that besides a members' list it contained a listing of conference rooms. "This is because they have a telephone number for each conference room in New York," she explained the rationale of the list as relating to something "they" have. "Wow," one of the participants said, impressed, "they've got a lot of conference rooms."

Double-clicking the members' address book, Miri searched for the page of Idit, one of the training's participants. Her search failed, and Idit explained to her that she misspelled her last name: "It's spelled Kipori, with a 'K,' not Tzipori like it is pronounced," she said. "How come it's spelled like that?" another participant inquired. Idit answered that her grandfather did not know how to spell the name in English; he made a mistake and it stuck. Her answer was followed by two jokes. One participant said, "Why is there a Japanese launderette in New York that is called Moshe Goldberg? Well, when the Japanese owner came to register his business, he stood behind a Moshe Goldberg. When it was his turn to register, the clerk asked him for his name and he said Sam Ting (same thing)." Adding to the laughter from this joke, another participant said: "A Jewish American came up to a Chinese man and slapped him on the face. The Chinese asked: 'What is that for?' The Jew answered, 'This is for Pearl Harbor.' 'But those were the Japanese!' the Chinese cried, and the Jew replied, 'Chinese, Japanese, what's the difference!' So the Chinese walked up to the Jew and slapped him on the face. 'What is that for?' the Jew asked. The Chinese answered, 'This is for *Titanic.*' 'But that was an iceberg,' said the Jew, and the Chinese replied, 'Iceberg, Rosenberg, what's the difference!'" These two Jewish name-jokes—both deriving humor from identity mistakes—seemed to express the fact that personal names have a broad, collective meaning. The jokes thus added a challenging twist to the joint intranet address book: the symbolic depiction of individual separateness and detachment (see previous scene) was offset by jokes implying that members belonged to a distinct collective with a bearing upon each other's most personal identities.

Laughter subsided and Miri surfed on. She arrived at a "Presentation Library" that belonged to the "Marketing" site. Browsing, she discussed the presentation documents and explained the ways that they could be put to use. "This offers you the possibility to see slides and summaries of corporate presentations," she explained. Gonen, a senior manager, asked who was responsible for the site. "New York are responsible for the corporate site," Miri answered. "I heard complaints that it is not updated," she added, answering an unstated complaint, "but they are still relevant and can be incorporated in new presentations."

Surfing back and forth, Miri double-clicked "Marketing" once again on the list of departments. Though jointly titled, this site turned out to be split into two when it came to products: there was one page for New York's product and another for Net (Isrocom's product). Yinon, one of the participants, asked, "It may be a petty comment, but why does New York's product always appear before Net?" This complaint about the ordering of the textual representation was met with nods of agreement around the table. "Remember that we took a ride on their existing system," Miri answered, expressing her own belonging to the local "we" while remaining loyal to her role as a representative of the global intranet team. "In the case of Customer Support," she added, further justifying the representational order that Yinon protested against, "they didn't have a site, and so Net appears first. It's purely technical." Her answer did not settle the issue. Apparently, there was a more general matter involved, and another participant named Gershon angrily said, "When you call our office in Beijing you hear 'Welcome to Amerotech of the Com group,' not 'Welcome to Globalint.'" This remark did not concern the intranet and Miri did not reply. Gonen, the senior manager, was the one to answer. Speaking as a representative of the formal system, he said: "This phone message was a strategic decision made in relation to only two places in the world." Gershon was hardly satisfied with this answer. "Perhaps strategic," he acknowledged the managerial rationale only to reject it, "but this message is heard in places that did not make a dime from sales of New York's product, just from sales of Net. There is something wrong here!" The enactment of a local organizational side—the "we" that has Net; the "we" that took a ride on "their" system—was thus accompanied by the enactment of a boundary that sliced through that side, delineating the strategies of management on one hand, and the sense of justice and local-patriotism of a subordinate on the other.

Miri continued to intranet surf, showing the participants the various sites and offering navigation tips. After a while, she arrived at the "Proposal Boilerplates" site. Gonen the manager warned: "These proposal boilerplates are very dangerous. They can never be sent unedited to clients." Ziv, one of his subordinates, complained that, "There have to be some good boilerplate versions that can be sent out." Miri nodded in agreement. "We've received these from New York," she said, refusing to take the blame. "They are so formatted that it is impossible to use them." Then, as she went on, she suddenly remembered a piece of gossip. "I heard that Jeff Ross quit, by the way," she said, referring to a member of Amerotech's Marketing. Some looks of curiosity were exchanged around the table and Gonen offered more in support of this piece of news from abroad: "Yeah," he said, "I read about this in an email." "I talked to New York," Miri said, defining the source of her gossip in this generalized, collective form, and thus re-rooting the information that flowed across boundaries in a phrase that sustained them, "and they told me about this."

Miri now pointed at the screen, turning her audience's attention to the site that was projected on it. This was the last site of her presentation, and it was called "Present Order." It contained images and descriptions of a long list of presents that could be ordered for suppliers, customers, and, under certain conditions, members. "Here is something really nice that New York did," Miri complimented her generalized teammates, "it is possible to order each item right here." "I saw this," a participant said with a humorous tone that seemed to trivialize the compliment. Cynically referring to a sport that is very peripheral in Israel but central in and quite symbolic of the United States, he said, "You can order golf balls with Globalint's name on it."

After the training was over, I stayed for some time, taking advantage of the opportunity to ask Miri some more questions about the intranet. Referring to its various sites, she explained that there was a division of labor between Isrocom and Amerotech with regard to their maintenance. "When I open the Corporate Communication site I am actually in New York," she said. "For Customer Support, they connect to us." "Furthermore," she went on to explicate the power that the intranet technology offers those who produce these organizational representations, "some sites are completely split. Take Human Resources, for example. It has three parts: one that only New York can see, one that only we can see, and one part that is for everybody to see." Answering my question concerning the logic of this arrangement, she explained: "Why should the people from New York see that we get three hundred dollars for clothing every five trips abroad? It doesn't exist over there. And in New York you have to stay only one year in a position before you can request a promotion. Here you need two years. This way Israelis cannot see New York's policies and vice versa."

Thus, the intranet was deliberately structured, it appears, to give an impression of unity while concealing difference and distinctions. Nevertheless, while it was intentionally designed this way, those who participated in the training interpreted the intranet texts from the point of view of a distinct group. Thus, Miri, the presenter, specified to her audience which intranet texts were under the responsibility of "New York" and which were not. Moreover, the way that her listeners referred to these texts implied a sense of a bounded belonging; a local collective and an organizational side with a joint concern for defending the relative status of Isrocom and its product inside the global system. As was the case of reactions to verbal and visual representations, however, this sense of collectivity did not override internal distinctions, especially between Gonen the manager and his subordinates, and also between Miri, a representative of the global intranet team, and her local audience.

Conclusions

The verbal, visual, and textual representations were all characterized by the same basic identity construction process. In all of them, a representation of non-present merger partners as being, in one way or another, bound together with locals was met with counter-representations of both division and diversity. Thus here too, as in the case of the communication events described in the previous chapter, both a global and a local version of an organizational identity came into play, as did a group of other, multiple identities—religious, genderial, hierarchical, and so forth. Strikingly, however, here members did not hold these multiple identities at bay, and there appeared to be no pervasive collective effort to publicly gloss over internal distinction. In fact, in some cases members seemed to celebrate local differentiations and variety. In the absence of the merger partners, in other words, the "public face" (Cohen 1986: 13; 1985) of Isrocom members' oneness had to a large degree been dissolved.

Moreover, in each of the three kinds of representations, politics and power seemed to bear upon the process of identity construction. In the scenes dealing with verbal representations—"Moshe's Tricks," "Pizza, Coke, and the Politics of Difference," and "Toast!"—politics was most evidently linked to the local version of the organizational identity, turning it into a site where personal interests assume collective significance. A member asking for social recognition, a manager demanding compliance, and an executive seeking to inspire motivation had each rendered merger partners a distinct "them," constructing their representation in dichotomous terms that were consistent with and thus seemed to endorse the notion of a distinct and separate organizational identity. Interestingly, however, this politically stimulated, polarizing talk was encountered by somewhat reserved reactions. The listeners—Yuval and I in the hallway, Ido in the R&D review, and the audience at the New Year celebration—did not challenge the enacted local boundary but also did not embrace it in a way that overruled an underlying irony: the fact that the content of such identity-talk—the notion of distinct, internal oneness—was incongruent with the condition of its enactment—internal interests and status differentiations.

In contrast, in the scenes dealing with visual and textual representations, power and politics were most evidently linked not to the local but to the global version of the organizational identity. In the snapshot displays and in the intranet texts ("The Kosher Lobster," "Image Games," and "Surfing the Organizational Cyber Space,") formal power came into play in organizationally sponsored displays of the merger partners as an integral and harmonious part of the "us." These global, formal displays were, in turn, encountered with resistant members who utilized parody, games, and jokes to invalidate any notion of an overall concerted collective, pointing out multiple identity distinctions—observant/nonobservant, managerial/subordinate, men/women, Israeli/American—and overshadowing global depictions with a sense of variety and difference. However, since the same sense of diversity that challenged managerial definitions of global unity also challenged definitions of local unity, here too, as in verbal representations, the process of demarcating members of the "them" simultaneously invalidated the internal unity of members of the "us." Thus, the site of power play was perhaps different than the one characteristic of the verbal representation scenes, but the overall process and effect seemed the same.

This account of the way in which power and politics came into play in identity-constituting representations leads to two conclusions. First, in the absence of Amerotech's members, global and local organizational identities as well as the pool of other, non-organizational identities became a form of discursive field: a system of meaning in which knowledge about the organization and membership within it was produced in a strategic and politically induced way. In this field, the various identities—each encircling a different collectivity and laying distinctive claims of commitment upon people—were invoked by social actors as a means for affecting other members: gaining their recognition, monitoring their behavior, inciting their motivation, shaping their perception, and so forth.

Second, and somewhat conversely, while power was thus involved in the production of identity through representation, it did not determine it in any final or fixed way. If anything, it set meaning in motion: in all of the scenes a representation of a global option was followed by a counter-representation that resisted it but also infused the local option with tension. In other words, power—whether invested in the global or the local version of the organizational identity, whether formal or informal—produced not only a meaning for identity but also a space where resistant meanings could emerge (Foucault, 1980). Indeed, it seems that since power in organizations (and beyond them) is never uniform, it lives in inherent tension with any notion of identity that it produces, contradicting any representation of unity and oneness—be it, in this case, the global "us" or the resistant local "us"—that it seeks or serves to promote. In other words, power does not settle issues of meaning, nor does it bring them to any final stop.

These findings are inconsistent with mainstream theory of organizational identity. As Chapter 1 suggests, many organizational theorists take the singularity and dominance of the managerial version of this identity for granted. However, the scenes that have been depicted indicate that management does not have enough power to define this identity for its members. Although it does seem to hold some potent means of representation—speeches, images, texts—it cannot finalize or determine the way that these are interpreted and reacted to. In Derrida's terms (for example, 1981), they cannot fix the relationship between the (identity-)signifiers and their referents: while aiming for closure, final meanings are always delayed, deferred, leaving an interpretive space within which the managerially sanctioned, as any, representation of identity (in this case the global as opposed to the local "us") can be endlessly disrupted or subverted and new meanings generated. Whatever medias management controls, it lacks control over all of them—most notably that of talk—and there are always ways for members to react to managerial representations and to construct alternative ones. At most, the managerial version of the organizational identity thus becomes one among several alternative representations that allow movement and flow in the discursive field.

The findings of this chapter are also incongruent with cross-cultural theories of global organizations. The notion that intercultural gaps embody that which is "problematic" about national identity in global organizations cannot account for the fact that national identity continued to have an impact even in the absence of Americans, during times completely devoid of intercultural interactions. Here, as in communication events, what seemed to be of consequence was the symbolic significance of national identity rather than any preexisting and stable cognitive essence that it supposedly imprinted in members' minds: a war shelter acting as a meeting room, a public holiday celebrated as an organizational event, repeated references to the merger partners as "the Americans," games attempting to discern "Americanness" from photographed images, a cynical remark about golf balls, and so forth. What seemed of weight here, in short, was the meaning attached to national identity; the way it was symbolically utilized by members rather than the way it cognitively impinged upon them.

On the whole, the findings of this chapter and the findings of the previous chapter add up to a complex conclusion. Within Isrocom, organizational life was replete with processes of identity construction. During the course of interactions with their merger partners and during the course of interactions amongst themselves, Isrocom's members actively delineated their separateness from Amerotech's members, securing it through exclusion, anchoring it along the seemingly objective, pre-existing national boundary, and challenging any representational depiction of global unity. Yet this enactment of a distinct and locally bounded organizational "us" was always partial, never going so far as to completely shatter the global-organizational identity and even incorporating it as a part of a discursive field. Additionally, this enactment was also partial with regard to other, non-organizational identities that rose to the surface and challenged not only the formal, global definition of unity but also the continually enacted local and resistant one. The process of identity construction was thus a dynamic process, one in which enacting a separate and distinct circle of organizational belonging entailed its own challenges and threats of demise. As it was innately incomplete, it seemed to demand a continual definitional effort on the part of members, and, indeed, in both the presence and absence of the merger partners members were generally engaged in a local identity project that was continuous and ongoing. Part II will deal with the question of how this definitional effort bore upon their other definitions of self.

PART II

The Merger and the Worker:
Aligning Identities, Centering Selves

CHAPTER 5

Israeli Identity

Mimicked Americanness
Surpassing Its Origin

Gabi, an engineer with a long career at Isrocom, occupied a spacious corner office of the kind reserved for senior managers. The walls of his office revealed information about him. The large bulletin board that hung above his desk contained many pictures of his sons and wife. All of the photographed family members wore the customary clothes of observant Jews, skullcaps in the case of the boys and a long skirt and a hat in the case of their mother. A second bulletin board contained pictures of Net, Isrocom's product, and newspaper clippings with reports of the company's achievements. A sketch board hung on another wall, and on the day that I visited the office it displayed a hand-drawn system design. Above the sketch board was a photograph of an Israeli desert and next to it a large map of the world. On another picture that displayed a puzzle with a piece of it separated from the whole, a hand-signed message from the CEO stated, "Thanks for being a part of the puzzle." In all these ways, the office bore evidence of who Gabi is: a manager, a father, a husband, a religious Jew, an engineer, an Israeli, a global worker, an appreciated member of Isrocom. In other words, it bore evidence of his multiple identities.

In a way, these multiple identities coexist only on the joint wall space. In actual interactions, they would lose the link of simultaneity and be presented in a situationally selective way, readily alternating from social context to social context, from interaction to interaction, in accordance with the specific partners to social exchange (Goffman 1959). In this sense, Gabi's walls did not represent who he is as much as the things that he could, at the right moment, be; the things that he could convince the others with whom he interacts that he has become (Van Maanen 1979: 96). His multiple identities are, in short, a repertoire of shifting and flexible displays; a behavioral range of sorts.

According to some postmodernist writers, multiplicity dominates the contemporary sense of self. Losing the support of traditional social arrangements, relationships in our time invite people to play out an unprecedented variety of roles. This variety makes it increasingly evident that any sense of a "true" or "authentic" self a person might have is merely a figure of a cultural imagination belonging, more and more, to the past (for example, Gergen 1991). In other words, in this view, fragmented social conditions accentuate multiplicity to such an extent that they move it from the realm of display to the realm of consciousness. Pulled in a myriad of identity-directions, people let go of even the illusion of coherence. Accordingly, the notion of an "integrated self," of a sterling convergence of identities,[1] is withering away.

And yet Part I of this book offered preliminary evidence that, at least as far as Isrocom's members are concerned, coherence is not so easily let go. In fact, in the scenes that have been depicted, coherence was actively, albeit not always successfully, attempted. Members' participation in the continual construction process of a separate, locally bounded organizational identity often involved the social-monitoring of other identities that rose to the fore: national identities, professional identities, hierarchical identities, immigrant identities, religious identities, and so forth. In other words, multiplicity was apparent but to a large extent controlled: the process of construction, I claimed, entailed the collective "centering" of members' "decentered" selves.

How, I now ask, did members experience these "centered" identities? How did they make sense of their own multiplicity in the context of such a dominant process of enacting the separate organizational "us"? What meanings did the purveyors of the locally bounded organizational identity attribute to these other identities that repeatedly emerged in the course of global work-life? How did they manage interrelation between their own different attachments in the face of the ongoing struggle to distinguish themselves from the merger partners?

In an attempt to offer a broad account of the issue of identities in Isrocom and to explore more thoroughly their interrelations, Part II of this study seeks to answer these questions. Focusing on those identities that seemed most salient—the Israeli identity (this chapter) and occupational and hierarchical work identities (the next chapter)—it shifts attention from the external, social setting in which the local-organizational identity was enacted, to the internal, personal setting in which it was to bear upon other definitions of self. Relying upon interviews rather than participant observations as the main source of data, it offers an analysis of members' talk and reflections and undertakes an inquiry into the ways they made sense of themselves and their others in the context of Isrocom's global merger.

Thus we begin: in the chapter that follows, I offer some general background about the Israeli identity and then go on to examine how members constructed it in the shadow of struggle between the organizational "us" and "them." Furthermore, as will later be explained, the Jewish identity is tightly related to and in some ways an integral part of the Israeli identity, and thus, to offer a more comprehensive account, members' construction of this identity will also be referred to in a separate section.

The Israeli Identity

Generally, the construct "Israeli identity" was originally forged by the cultural and political elite that ruled the country in its early decades. Israel, established in 1948 and formed out of waves of Jewish immigration from various countries, was originally governed by a group consisting mostly of East European—"Ashkenazi"—Jews who immigrated during the pre-state years and their offspring. Energetically embracing a "melting pot" doctrine, the Ashkenazi elite used state agencies such as schools, youth movements, public media, and the military for a cultural project of fundamentally resocializing the heterogeneous mass of post-1948 Jewish immigrants consisting, for the most part, of Holocaust survivors and Jews from Arab countries (Kimmerling 2001). Their goal was a unified national identity encompassing all but the marginalized Arab citizens who were excluded from it from the start. Built upon a conscious negation of the historical image of the religious, passive, nonproductive, and defenseless Diaspora Jew (Raz-Krakotzkin 1994; see also Katriel 1986), the "new Israeli" was to speak a modernized Hebrew and become a "normalized," secular, Westernized, and industrious person.

While still influential, the Ashkenazi elite has, in the past two or three decades, lost its hold on various centers of power. Concurrently, its hegemonic "Israeliness" project has to a large extent been undermined. The underlying pluralism of Israeli society (Smooha 1978) is no longer contained, and, along with a new ethnic vitality (Weingrod 1985), internal political tensions that have heightened since the 1967 Occupation of the West Bank and Gaza, and multiple citizenship discourses (Shafir & Peled 2002), it is increasingly slicing through any unified image of collective identity. As Kimmerling (2001: 2) observes, "within the Israeli state, a system of cultural and social plurality is emerging, but in the absence of a concept or ideology of multiculturalism." Indeed, "Israeli identity" has become an arena of political and cultural strife in which various groups continually struggle for dominance in defining it and securing their place within it (for example, Regev 2000; Shohat 1989).

All this is but a very general background designed to negate any naïve notion or misconceived impression of a coherent national identity, tailor-made and ready for wear by Isrocom's members. In fact, national identities never are. "Modern nations," writes Hall (1996: 617), "are all cultural hybrids," their implied unity a "discursive device" that obscures internal divisions and differences by representing them as unified. While perhaps linked to a powerful arsenal of (often conflicting) images or versions of "oneness"—totalizing but inherently ambivalent and incomplete "narrations" (Bhabha, 1990), which enable the nation to be "imagined" as a single community (Anderson 1983)—national identity has no final meaning, no moment of absolute truth. Its fixity is in this sense unfixed, its unity un-unified, and both need an other, an "outside," in order to assume the shape of a quintessential "inside."

Nowhere, however, is the inside/outside boundary of Israeliness more incomplete, more Janus-faced and unsettled, than in relation to America.[2] Politically and economically dependent upon the United States, Israelis often joke that Israel is the 51st state of America, an outpost of Western democracy in the Middle East. Adopting American values, symbols, and codes of conduct in various spheres of life, Israeli society has been undergoing extensive processes of "Americanization," its cultural fabric becoming deeply ingrained with a commercial, instrumental, technological, and rational mindset that expresses itself in both social organization forms and discursive practices (for discussions see, for example, Ram 2004; Frenkel & Shenhav 2003; Azaryahu 2000).[3] This prevalence of America and things American in Israel has led to reactions ranging from that of conservative streams who traditionally "felt threatened by 'decadent Westernized and Americanized' culture," fearing that it "would take over 'Jewish society' and transform Israel into 'just another nation,'" (Kimmerling 2001: 55), to that of secular and predominantly Ashkenazi streams who look upon the West as a cultural ideal. Seeking to repress oriental social sectors and oriental aspects of the Jewish identity, even at the price of accepting a stigmatized self-image as a flawed model of modern "high" culture (Khazzoom 2003), these latter groups have been committed to a concept of self-improvement that is defined by Western role models, in particular the United States. Indeed, this process has been so total and robust that thousands of Israelis have been unable to resist "the magic pull of America." According to Sobel (1986), most of those who migrated from Israel left for a chance to live the seductive American "real thing" rather than its peripheral and pale version.

How, then, did members make sense of Israeliness in the context of a resistant, local-organizational identity project constituted against representatives of this so-called "high" culture? What, if any, notion of distinguishing national unity, what versions of "oneness," were deployed in the midst of a social-struggle against the managerial attempt to fuse an American "real thing" with a predominantly Israeli organizational universe? The next two sections will address these questions. Identifying two underlying themes in members' references to nationality—that of a collective personality template and that of shared social status—the sections will bring to light the inherent ironies and paradoxes that were involved in members' constructions of national identity in Isrocom.

A Template of a Personality: National Identity as a Stereotype

The first major theme underlying perceptions of national identity in the field was a personality theory of sorts. Despite the fact that Isrocom's members were not in any way a homogenous group—the ethnic, secular/religious, and class diversity characteristic of Israeli society was prevalent here too—in their accounts "Israeli identity" was stripped of any hint of diversity and conflict. Generally, it was used to convey a sense of deep and pre-existing commonality, one that was defined in terms of a shared bundle of traits and seen to manifest itself in the work setting in typical ways. These manifestations, furthermore, were cast in a polarized positive and negative form: it was members' perception that Israeli identity is the source of things good or bad in the local, Isrocom "us"; of merits or faults that rendered their local organization either superior or inferior in relation to the American merger partner. While the positive and negative conceptions related to the Israeli identity were often intermingled, at times expressed within the same interview, the positive conception was much more common, expressed in practically all of the interviews. Indeed, the negative conception seemed somewhat of an exception to a general rule.[4] Despite the relative low frequency of its expression, however, it did seem significant and worth reporting in the sense of representing an essential distinction in the orientation of Isrocom's members toward their national belonging in this global context. Accordingly, in what follows, both of these conceptions are documented.

The Israeli Identity as Organizational Merit

References to the Israeli identity as a source of work-related virtue were characterized by one central claim. Constructing it in terms of essential characteristics, members idealized their national identity by claiming that, in comparison to the American identity of the merger partners, it marks a greater fit to organizational interests, goals, and values.

More specifically, members claimed that Israeli identity imbues them with an ability to disregard various "obstacles" that limit the Americans' contribution to the organization. An example of such an obstacle was temporal conventions. An engineer illustrates:

> Most people (here) have 10 to 20 extra work hours a week. Managers have 30 to 40 extra hours a month. There are also people who work 260 hours a month. (But)

they work differently . . . only 9:00 to 6:00. This is the Americans, this is their work style. In Israel we are crazy when it comes to work.

In this citation, the engineer constructs national identity as the collective source of a distinctive working-hour pattern, juxtaposing the alleged boundaryless or "crazy" temporal dedication of Israelis with that of "the Americans." A customer-support engineer articulates a similar contrast, once again conjuring up Israeli identity as the source of temporally unbound commitment:

> If you carefully analyze the character of Israelis, their habits . . . their dedication and how much they are willing to sacrifice in order to succeed in their jobs and achieve progress, then you'll find a huge difference. Americans need their weekends, their freedom, normal hours. . . . They don't commit themselves to things that in order to succeed in them you practically have to commit suicide.

Note the pervasive metaphor that is used to depict the professed boundarylessness of the Israeli devotion to the organization: willingness to "commit suicide."

Distinctions of temporal dedication were not only associated with work hours. The constructed difference between the "us" and the "them" also concerned other matters, such as the strictness of deadline-discipline. "Generally, with regard to everything," said, for example, an economic analyst, "deadlines don't mean the same to the Americans as they do to us. They don't kill themselves for deadlines. People (here) go crazy in order to meet deadlines." Another related matter was the work-family balance. A senior manager illustrates:

> They don't work hard. I mean, the Americans don't work 12, 13 hours a day. . . . The American—his first loyalty from the first moment to the last is to the family. . . . The sacrifice and dedication that you see here is higher than you see there. This isn't new. We've seen this in another American company that we work with.

Here too, then, national generalizations are used to anchor and solidify the sense of contrast and local virtue—the locals' dedication versus "the Americans'" reserve. Articulating a contrast in terms of a characteristic hierarchy of loyalties between work and family, the manager claims that Americans turn their personal lives into an obstacle that stands between them and the organization's best interest.

Moreover, it wasn't just personal lives, but also personal interests. Reproducing the basic construct to other spheres of discourse, members attributed to Americans the tendency to put their own interests before those of the company. As an illustration, a marketing engineer offers an account of a trip abroad:

The Americans like to spend more money. They like to spend a lot more money. For example they fly business all the time. Once we (me and a colleague from Amerotech) had a client-meeting that was scheduled for 9 a.m. in India. I arrived at 1 a.m., and when I left the hotel in the morning I saw this huge Mercedes parking outside (laughs). I always take cabs over there. I never order a Mercedes. I always take the local cabs. They are the kind of cars that were driven in Israel during the 50s. Funny cars. But I have no problem, I take them in good spirit. And he (the colleague) orders a Mercedes! It probably costs the company a fortune, but he . . . it is American, simply American. He takes a Mercedes.

Note in this citation how the marketing engineer frames a specific instance as an illustration of a general type. This way, the contrast becomes objectified, and the single encounter is assembled as "proof" of an underlying, nationally determined essence.

Moreover, there were other personal interests that members assembled this way. "For an American the issue of ranks and titles is much more important," declared for example a worker from marketing, and, adding sarcasm to the comparison, an engineer said: "They take their titles very seriously. Everybody has a title. Here we don't have the title issue. If someone is a Director, what am I supposed to do? Bow down when I enter his room? Shine his shoes?" Similarly, in the following citation a senior manager depicts the merger partners as "spoiled," claiming that, in contrast to Israelis, they try to avoid risking themselves for the sake of the organization:

There are differences . . . like their unwillingness to travel to places that are so called more dangerous. They are much more spoiled than we are, that's what it looks like. (Which places?) Places which are dangerous because of internal wars or personal safety problems. (Israelis are less so?) Yes. It's not surprising. People know that even when South Lebanon is bombed people still enjoy themselves in restaurants in Tel Aviv. When they see it here they know that it exists in other places. And don't forget that everyone here completed military service. Exposure to dangers of this kind is less frightening for Israelis. It is very natural for Israelis.

Thus, paradoxically, local dangers are presented here as leading to global courage, creating workers who "naturally" disregard personal hazards during their engagement in global organizational missions.[5]

And the list of distinctions went on: the same basic construct—polarized national generalizations anchoring a sense of work-related contrast—was colored in infinite shades as it was reproduced across the organizational discourse. Thus, it was not only safety risks that Americans were claimed to avoid, but also decision-making risks. More specifically, members' generalizations also depicted a collective American fear of taking responsibility for decisions. Israelis were again portrayed in opposite terms. A public relations worker illustrates the American side of this contrast:

> There are things that are related to the general culture, Israelis and Americans. It is expressed in work, their insistence on procedures, on paperwork, their fear of making individual decisions. There always has to be some Daddy who tells you, 'Yes, that's okay.'

And a human resource worker depicts the Israeli side of this contrast:

> My impression is that Israelis work faster and that we take more responsibility for risks. For example, if there is a certain issue on the agenda then I will take responsibility for it. If I will get in trouble for it then I will get in trouble, if I won't then I won't, but I will make the decision, and I will update whoever is relevant and that's that. I think that in the Americans' case everything demands consensus, consultations, information gathering, bla, bla, bla.

Note again how a single instance is presented as an illustration of a general type: the HR worker's self-characterization is assembled as "proof" of an underlying, national essence.

Moreover, in members' constructions Americanness was not only said to inhibit the taking of risks but also the attainment of goals. Articulating yet another contrast, members claimed that the American identity imbues members with a mental tendency to stick to and elaborate formal work procedures, while Israelis are committed to the goal rather than to the details of the process. An engineer speaks of this difference, framing the Israelis' side of the contrast as the privileged norm:

> We work here like we worked in the army. We have a goal and we have to accomplish it, the quicker the better. . . . It is an Israeli characteristic. All of us together for a very clear, marked-off goal. For Americans the process is important, how things will be managed, ordered. The goal is clear but they don't fight for it. They approach it, but they do not charge toward it.

Note the utilization of military terminology. Broadly, the military is quite central in Israeli society and, despite some resistant voices that have lately been heard, its legitimacy is widely accepted (see Lomsky-Feder & Ben-Ari 1999; Kimmerling 2001). This "military-mindedness" (Kimmerling 2001) is both expressed in and reinforced by the mandatory conscription of almost all Jewish men and women,[6] the tendency to view military service as a sign of civic and personal virtue, and the disposition to turn it into a major building block of identity-constructs (Sasson-Levy 2002). Phrases such as "all of us together for the goal," "fighting for the goal," and "charging forward," all of which are a part of widespread military jargon, should be read in this context, namely as local symbols of the virtues of dedication, collective commitment, and a willingness for self-sacrifice. The use of military connotations thus constitutes a powerful symbolic "pick" from the arsenal of images of Israeli oneness, further rooting the sense of overruling distinction in something external and predetermined.

The alleged procedural orientation was related to other American "faults" that members accused their merger partners of; to other forms of "obstacles" that hold them back. For example, a marketing engineer constructs a notion of obsessive planning:

> They are not willing to work until everything is organized in advance. It holds the schedule back. With Israelis this would never happen. We are used to working without a pre-organized schedule. Maybe it is like this because of the army, maybe it originates from other places . . . they really do need everything to be organized. It is like a TV cooking show: they begin working only after everything is organized in little dishes, like soldiers. It doesn't matter that at home you take a spoon of sugar from the shelf and that's all there is to it. That's the way that they are. They need everything to be organized in advance.

A manager from the HR Department makes another related distinction, attributing to "the Americans" an inflexibility of thought and framing it as something that hinders goal attainment:

> I like Americans much less than I did before and before I wasn't too crazy about them either. . . . I discovered things that I had heard about in the past from people who worked with the United States. I had the opportunity to discover them for myself. (Like what?) I found out that they are very rigid, very inflexible, very square—very, very square. I mean, the system, the method always comes before the idea or the content . . . this is very burdensome.

Similarly, an economic analyst asserts difference in creativity between the Israeli and American character, linking it to the issue of orderliness:

> The Americans—in their character they are more square, they are less creative. They are used to living in ordered frames. . . . They are organized. Look at how their streets are built.

And an R&D manager refers to improvisations, ascribing to Americans the realization that the character associated with Israeli identity is better in this regard:

> Israelis have many advantages that Americans like: the fact that we are more direct, quicker, more daring, all of our improvisations. Americans don't know how to do this. They like this in Israelis because this leads to solutions. They don't know how to do this. Their thinking is very, very square . . . it is difficult for them

to break through their thinking mode into other directions. And I think that they like it a lot in Israelis.

Thus, using national attributions for fixing boundaries, naturalizing distinctions, and typecasting the merger partners as less worthy organizational members, members spoke of Israeli identity as the origin of a direct goal-orientation and a flexible mind. In contrast, American identity was constructed as implying a procedure-orientation that redirects attention away from organizational goals toward documentation and leads to overly rigid, wastefully detailed, inflexible, uncreative, overly ordered, and evasive thought, planning, and decision-making processes.

Another obstacle that members assembled in their accounts was structural formalities. Illustrative of this is a comment by an engineer who used religious terminology to declare that:

> They are very submissive to authority. The word of the boss is the word of God. . . . Our perception is that what the manager says is important and that it has to be seriously considered, but if he does not seem reasonable or if we think that he is wrong then it is legitimate to come out and say that it isn't right, or that it doesn't seem right. . . . That's the Israeli character. It doesn't exist as much in their character.

Thus, according to this engineer "the Israeli character" enables Israelis to overlook formal hierarchical boundaries when these set limits to their organizational contribution while the merger partners sanctify them.

Furthermore, members also maintained that the alleged Israeli indifference to hierarchical distinctions cuts both ways. According to them, not only do Israeli subordinates typically express themselves without restraint, but Israeli managers are much more attentive than their American counterparts, not allowing formalities or concerns for deference to obscure their commitment to organizational goals. A marketing engineer illustrates this claim with regard to "escalations," an English-titled, semi-formal, and widespread process of voicing complaints up levels of hierarchy. He refers to Sayeret Matkal, a small, elite military unit that symbolizes the myth of the Israeli spirit; of its alleged ability to withstand mighty enemies through dedication to collective goals and witty resourcefulness:

> I would say that as Israelis we work like Sayeret Matkal. Things are more formal over there, and things can get stuck because of it. Over here a project manager can leave an urgent message for a senior R&D manager, to make an escalation, to yell at him that things are not working, that he won't have it. It is acceptable here. They don't have such a thing there. The senior manager would throw the project manager out of the room. He would see the door close behind him in a second.

Similarly, a technical writer conjures up more informal practices for channeling upward demands in Isrocom, assembling them as evidence of his nationally based distinction:

> Israelis are very informal. . . . It is less so in the case of Americans. They are very formal. Isrocom is characterized by complete informality, even in terms of managerial levels. I can go into Ofek's office (an Executive VP) and tell him whatever I like. And not only to Ofek, I can go into the office of anyone in Isrocom. There is total informality.

The structural obstacles that members referred to related not only to hierarchy but also to the definition of roles. According to Isrocom's members, Israeli identity imbues members with a tendency to take unlimited responsibilities upon themselves, far beyond their job descriptions. Americans, in contrast, were portrayed as limiting their involvement to the bounded zone of their formally defined authority and accountability. An industrial engineer asserts this difference, framing it as a cultural-gap:

> One of the basic cultural differences between them and us is the horizon of perspective. . . . Theirs is narrow and not long: I do not do what I haven't been told to do. In our case we look to do things that aren't defined.

Furthermore, members maintained that Israelis seek not only to do but also to know things that are beyond the scope of their role definitions. Thus says a worker from marketing:

> Israelis also have this tendency not to look at things from a limited perspective . . . to see things broadly. Their knowledge is not concentrated in one very specific area. It is broader knowledge. . . . A person who is working in one area can understand the person who sits next to him and who is working in another area. From what I know of Americans . . . I have a feeling that they have a tendency to focus. This is my area and this is what I know. If you want to know what is happening in that area, the person here next to me is the expert, so ask him. I don't have to know about this topic because I am not the expert on it. Knowledge has no breadth.

Going a step forward, members also linked this notion of a nationally based gap in perspectives to various characteristics of Israeli and American societies. A senior marketing manager offers an example. Note again how he constructs "causes" and picks "evidence" as a means for naturalizing the diametrical opposition:

> We have a broader perspective. I think it is a cultural result of living in the State of Israel. It is a small state. A lot of people travel abroad all the time, and we see in our news what is going on in the world. . . . What we are seeing with the Americans is that their perspective is not broad enough. I think that it also results from

. . . look at the news in the States: 95% of it is local. Not even national. Really local. What happened in the subway.

Finally, related to notions of Israeli informality and directness was an oft-cited distinction relating to cultural rules of expression. According to members, the Israeli identity implies a direct, perhaps even aggressively direct, uncensured, authentic, and unmediated character, one that exhibits no gaps between "true" and expressed views. On the other, polarized side of this generalization, they declared that, "the Americans don't say what they think"; that they don a polished social mask that manifests niceties but conceals true attitudes and intent. An industrial engineer illustrates:

> I think that they are very, very nice. But with Americans niceness involves many question marks because there is a lot of hypocrisy in it. The hypocritical thing is that they always say, 'Everything is okay, everything is okay.' That's the general atmosphere even when things are not okay. And that's different from us. In our case when something is not okay it will be immediately observable upon us.

A customer support manager offers another example:

> Lack of response is typical of Americans. . . . Instead of dealing with a problem they just, not exactly ignore it, but say 'Yes, yes, yes' and do nothing. There is an example for this: when they ask 'How are you?' they don't mean it. That's the difference between an Israeli 'How are you' and an American 'How are you.' And when an American says, 'It is wonderful' you can't know if he means it or not.

In sum, Isrocom's members spoke of the Israeli and American identities in terms of common bundles of traits; of predetermined personalities. Reducing people "to a few, simple, essential characteristics which are represented as fixed by Nature" (Hall 1997: 257), these national stereotypes were used to solidify the sense of inter-group boundary. As far as their own group was concerned, the Israeli identity was claimed to imply a personality that is not held back, one that is not committed to any social, structural, cultural, or personal boundaries that limit involvement with and commitment to the organization. Framed through contrasts to the American identity of the merger partners, the Israeli cluster of traits was repeatedly presented as manifesting less distance from and greater fit to organizational interests and ideals. Indeed, since nearly every possible aspect of organizational life—temporal discipline, authority relations, role commitment, goal orientation, job dedication, and so forth—was placed under the umbrella of the Israeli/American dichotomy, this binary, oppositional construct was reproduced to endless dimensions of organizational discourse, and an endless array of "examples" was assembled to augment its persuasive effect. Conceptualized in terms of a causal scheme that links stereotypical traits to generalized work-related merits, national identity became the anchor of a moral connotation that members used to privilege the local organizational "us" and to naturalize its distinctiveness.

Not all, however, was positive. As claimed, while in practically all of the interviews members referred to an Israeli cluster of traits and framed it as the origin of organizational merit, in some cases they also spoke of it as relating to some unattractive traits. Such references will be discussed next.

The Israeli Identity as Organizational Faults

In relatively few but nonetheless significant cases, members spoke as self-criticizers. Instead of idealizing themselves, they pointed out the faults of their organizational "us" and sought its improvement. Despite the difference in the moral tone, the professed origin of these faults was the same as that of organizational merits: the naturalized, solidified, stereotyped Israeliness. The tenets of such self-criticism, it seems, originated from contemporary Israeli discourse, some of them having slang titles. For example, a marketing manager cynically speaks of the Israeli identity as the origin of the unattractive trait of *partachiut*—Hebrew slang for a hurried, sloppy, and unprofessional work orientation—declaring it inferior to the work orientation typical of Americans:

> The American work method is the right method. We work in a *partachi* way. They work once and they release the final product. During the time that they work we release the product five times but it always comes out completely offside and then we are busy fixing it. . . . *Partachiut*—it is a science over here.

Referring to "The Achievers Club," an organizational practice that was imported from Amerotech in which members nominate "excellent" coworkers for a small "club" that offers special status and bonuses, an engineer talks of Israelis' inability to *lefargen,* to offer supportive, envy-less compliments. He speaks of the need to improve the local organization by overcoming its members' tendency to do so:

> The Achievers' Club program—I guess that we don't know how exactly to digest it. It is very un-Israeli. I think it is something that should be done, but I also think that more should be done to promote it. The response rate (here) was low, but it has to be given a chance. The problem is Israeliness. It is something that should be worked at, I mean it is very un-Israeli to *lefargen,* but still.

Discussing the locals' social orientation toward their merger partners, an industrial engineer speaks in a cynical, moral tone of self-condemnation of *shachtzanut tzabarit,* native-Israeli arrogance:

My feeling is that we have a problem with the Israeli character: we think that we know and understand everything. . . . I see it in our meetings with New York. When they came here in November (before the merger), we presented to them everything that we are doing and explained to them how we would work after the merger. There wasn't any consultation with them. In our defense it can be said that they said 'Yes, yes, yes,' they agreed to every word. It took me a while to understand that that's the American character. Americans always say yes, they never-ever say no. But there were cases in which they did try to sway us in their direction, and we overcame them with the *shachtzanut tzabarit*. . . . That's the Israeli arrogance: we know how to solve everything. We are the kings of solutions.

A manager explicates similar self-criticism when referring to Israelis' proclaimed pushiness and impoliteness:

I think that we are a little bit too pushy. We overrun them a little too much. . . . It doesn't grant us the love and respect of the Americans. . . . There are times during meetings in which I simply squirm in my chair, in which I feel uncomfortable. I am Israeli-born, a *tzabar*,[7] but it still bothers me—our attitude and all that.

In the following illustration the moral tone of criticism is heightened as a parallel is drawn between the merger situation and Israel's occupation of South Lebanon, binding together these two situations by the common Israeli fault of a conqueror's attitude:

I served as an officer in the army during the Lebanon war and everything, but it took me a while to understand what it means to be a conquering nation, what it means to occupy another nation. Were I among the conquered I too would have wanted to send us to hell. You've got to visit Amerotech to see that 99% of their identity has been erased. There is no Amerotech. It reminded me of Lebanon, how they signed a peace agreement with us, and then they murdered those who signed it, and we barely managed to get the hell out of there.

An industrial engineer offers yet another piece of moral self-criticism, tying Isrocom members' behavior to other alleged Israeli characteristics:

Dov's last trip to New York was under the title of (xxx) system planning. But in a conversation before they left, it was agreed that they would also try to learn (Amerotech's) processes in order to transfer their production here. We sent spies to steal information. This is what we actually did. We are Israelis, we have both the eagerness to dominate and the fear of persecution.

In sum, Isrocom's members did not always speak positively of their organization's characteristics. In some cases, they referred to faults and need for improvement and listed negative traits that supposedly permeate them by virtue of their Israeli origin. While relatively rare, these accounts are nonetheless significant in that they indicate the unintended consequences of members' construction efforts. More specifically, in the accounts the stereotypical, generalized, reductionist mode of conceptualizing national identity remained in place while its meaning began to slip away from the dominant identity project of Isrocom's members, no longer serving to aggrandize the status of the local "us," and instead bringing to mind submerged notions of flaw and weakness. In other words, the national personality construct, otherwise used to solidify the sense of an Isrocom-Amerotech contrast and privilege the "us," could not resist some negative connotations that "spoiled" the sense of local virtue.

As claimed, "Israeli identity" entailed an additional meaning for Isrocom's members besides a distinct personality. The next section will explore this second theme.

Global Marginality: The Israeli Identity as a Shared Status

For Isrocom's members "Israeli identity" also meant a shared, *subordinate* status defined in relation to some wider, global scheme of social hierarchy, a hierarchy that renders America and things American superior ideals.[8] Drawing parallels between the merger situation—a generally unique constellation in which Israelis were on the acquiring side[9]—and opposite hypothetical cases involving countries that were framed as Israel's inferiors, members presented the merger as a reversal of what was consequently asserted as the "natural," taken for granted social order. Following are two illustrations: in the first an Operations manager draws such a parallel involving Israel's neighbor Jordan, and in the second an R&D manager draws another parallel involving Cameroon.

> When I explain to my subordinates over here what is the meaning of the fact that we took over the business, I say, 'Imagine that a company from south Jordan would have taken over Com. Imagine that they would have come here to Tel Aviv to tell us what to do.' I think that it is not a bad example. If a company from Jordan, from, I don't know, (the city of) Irbid, would have taken over Isrocom in Tel Aviv, it would have been the same.

> For Americans this merger is . . . Well, it's just like a country like Cameroon would have acquired us.

In these citations, the managers define "the meaning" of the merger in terms of its relation to a global hierarchy whereby Israel has a specific place in the ranked order of things. The parallels that are drawn with Jordan and Cameroon are used to bolster the symbolic effect of the fact of a merger with Americans, pointing out and, at the same time, asserting the taken-for-grantedness of Israel's subordinate social status in relation to that of America. In other words, such hypothetical constructions, such reversal games that members designed as a means for conveying the uniqueness of the merger situation, marked their acknowledgement of the greater social prestige and standing of Americans in the wider social context.

Interestingly, this acknowledgement did not seem to undermine their organizational self-image, their broad sense of superior organizational worth inside Globalint. On the contrary, the notion of reversal imbued the fact of their Israeliness with a dramatic ambience, making their collective organizational attributes and accomplishments look somewhat more impressive and heroic: the Israelis of Isrocom had defeated the undefeatable, conquered the conquerors. Accordingly, there seemed to be some relish of poetic justice in their constructions of themselves, their American partners, and the merger situation that had brought them together. Rather than evading the issue of the general social superiority attributed to Americans, members repeatedly emphasized it, obviously perceiving it as something that further aggrandizes their own organizational value and achievements. Illustrative of this is the following citation of a marketing engineer:

> The American culture is a culture of winners. (They think) 'We are the Americans, we are the leaders, we are the leaders of the world.' . . . I think that in general we Israelis have much less of a problem working for an American company. We grow up inspired by American society. All the commercials in Israel, 'Sleep with Flannel blanket and feel America,' NBA basketball, everything that is broadcasted here implies that 'American' is good. . . . This is the message here. That's why there is no problem for an Israeli company to be owned by an American company. But people in the States (think): where is Israel anyway? What the hell is it? Who is an Israeli? What are his credentials?

A manager from Operations offers an even more extreme account of Americans' alleged unawareness of Israel, bolstering through this dramatized account the local side's achievement:

> It is a foreign company that took over an American company . . . a foreign company, not an English-speaking company, completely different. They were never exposed to Israeli culture. . . . Some people over there didn't even know how to spell 'Israel.'

An Executive VP talks in a similar vein, constructing a sense of poetic justice through an animated metaphor:

> They're probably thinking, 'Okay, so you guys know English, but when exactly did you get off the trees?' . . . (But) we made it clear to them that without the merger they would have collapsed.

The production manager who is cited next aggrandizes the local side's accomplishments by ascribing to the merger-partners the shock of realization that they had been overcome by those who were thought inferior but were proven superior:

> I assume that there is significance to the fact that an Israeli company acquired an American company. They were in shock when they came here, when they walked around. They saw the power, the scopes. They did not appreciate who is standing against them. I do not believe that Americans are used to being in a position of inferiority and here they were definitely acquired.

A finance manager offers a more colorful version of this proclaimed shock:

> Israeli management is like a sword-in-the-stomach for them. We are from the Middle East. It must have been very difficult for them.

Thus, members' declarations of organizational superiority within the merged company were accompanied by an underlying sense of a general social inferiority beyond its boundaries. Expressing a pre-existing model of global hierarchy, a map of cultural and social inequality, they promulgated dramatized images of the Americans' condescension toward and unfamiliarity with Israel and Israelis, as well as of their shock concerning the national identity of those who had taken them over. This talk had the effect of imbuing the story of the local "us" with an "against-all-odds" dramatic effect, one that served both to aggrandize the collective accomplishments of the local organization and to reaffirm its alleged superiority. In other words, for members, Israeli identity meant not only a preordained set of characteristics but also a general social inferiority that, through a paradoxical twist of meaning, bestowed further virtue upon its own organizational manifestation. Pre-existing notions of the general superiority of the Americans on the outside were thus inflected into a new direction whereby they were made to bolster the sense of virtue and accomplishment of the non-Americans on the inside.

The Jewish Question

A complex relationship exists between the Israeli and the Jewish identities. Israel is formally defined as a Jewish state that belongs to the "Jewish People" (including those who are not its citizens), and, as far as national symbols, formal rhetoric, and public institutions are concerned, the two identities are to a significant degree intertwined.[10] While Zionist nationalism to some degree detached Jewish symbols from their traditional content and granted them new meanings (Ben-Rafael 2005: 367), notions of nationality have generally remained anchored in religious values, symbols, and terms that transcend (but nevertheless live in tension with) Israel's self-definition as a secular democracy that is administered by universal laws (Kimmerling 2001). Thus, despite the fact that the majority of its Jewish-Israeli population is nonobservant,[11] the essence of Israeli society's right and reason to exist is still tightly embedded in religious symbols and texts and some sense of Jewish primordialism endures public debate and cultural conflict (Kimmerling 2001; see also Beit-Hallahmi & Sobel 1991).

Accordingly, the boundaries that distinguish Israel from other countries become somewhat blurred when other countries' Jewish citizens are concerned. While there is a divergence between Israeli Judaism and American (and other Diaspora-) Judaism (see Liebman & Cohen 1990), special formal and informal contacts, ties, bonds, and definitions of unity persist, reinforcing the Israeli/Jewish identity "package" to an extent that warrants the following question: how did Isrocom members make sense of the Jewish identity in the field? Were Amerotech's Jewish members rendered an "us" or a "them"? How, in other words, did this identity figure into the discourse of difference?

To begin with, members usually were aware of who among the merger partners was Jewish. According to their accounts, however, they never directly asked about religious beliefs: there were other reported ways of knowing, most typically gossip ("in the beginning," an interviewee told me, admitting gossip but also confining it to the past, "it was a topic that was discussed"); name inferences ("one of them is called Josh Cohen, so judging by his name you can't miss"); or self-identification by the Jewish members themselves ("Howard told me that he is Jewish and goes to temple"). Additionally, there were cases in which members claimed to have made a character inference. Enacting the Jewish identity as a form of in-between identity, members spoke of it as closely resonating with some of the traits that they attributed to themselves. A manager from Operations offers an example:

> It's not very difficult to find out who is Jewish among them . . . on the first meeting on that first day we understood who is the Jewish guy: Mark. Very quickly it became very clear who is the Jewish guy. In the beginning he did not say so but we felt it. He talked a little more, he interfered more, he expressed his opinions against those of his superiors. Then at dinner in the evening . . . he also said so. I don't ask such questions, we didn't ask—somehow it came out. But even before it came out it was clear to us that there was something odd here. On that first day it was already clear that he is Jewish.

Note in this account how Jewish identity is depicted in a way that echoes with and thus reaffirms the personality theory attributed to national identity in the field. Namely, Jewish identity is presented as a highly visible trait-cluster closely resembling the trait-cluster attributed to Israeliness. And still, for members the difference that mattered was the national, not religious, one. A VP says:

There are differences between an American Jew and an American non-Jew. I felt it in the past when I lived there, I saw the differences. But there is still a greater difference between an Israeli and an American Jew.

Thus, members both enacted Amerotech's Jews as an in-between category and insisted upon the underlying validity and overruling significance of the national dichotomy. There was, in other words, a hierarchy of distinctions in which the religious was subordinated to the national. Accordingly, despite the fact that Jewish identity was something that was talked about, inferred, learned, and mapped out, it was explicitly rendered immaterial to definitions of work situations and unimportant workwise. "Knowing," as one member said, "didn't change our relationship with them." And, in the words of another: "Work relations with them have nothing to do with the fact that they're Jewish." A marketing manager even went so far as to declare Jewishness not only irrelevant and unimportant but also a disadvantage in the global work context:

> Jewishness is never an issue. You know what? In the area of the world that I am working in it is a limitation to be a religious Jew. If I had to consider it, and I feel uneasy to say so, but if I had two good candidates, one a religious Jew and one not, I would take the latter. In Vietnam, for example, they work on Saturdays. It is a workday. . . . In many places all over the world it is acceptable to go out to dinner, but there are no kosher restaurants in Vietnam. Flights are also a problem for people who do not fly on Saturday. There are many limitations. So in our area of work it is a problem to be Jewish.

In sum, the Jewish identity of members from Amerotech was something that was known but denied a place in definitions of work situations. While it was for some a sort of in-between trait cluster, members explicitly disallowed it to interfere in or obscure the basic Israeli-American dichotomy. They sought to find out and they made known who among the merger partners was Jewish, but they also declared this piece of information irrelevant and even illegitimate. The Jewish identity, in short, was basically rendered a gossip identity in the field; an identity that was rhetorically marginalized in relation to the national discourse and thus prevented from interfering with the binary postulation of local identities.

Conclusions

The social construction of a separate, local-organizational identity within Globalint was accompanied by repeated references to nationality. These references conjured up an image of Israeli identity as stamping a pre-existing, homogenous, and distinctly un-American personality template onto individual members. Usually, members ascribed to this personality template a positive value that privileged them as superior or "purer" manifestations of organizational ideals. Claiming that it assimilates an unmediated, direct, and highly dedicated character to Israelis, they described it through metaphors of boundarylessness and contrasted it to the "constrained" character of "the Americans." At the same time, members also ascribed to their national identity an inferior social status defined in relation to a global scheme of social hierarchy. Through a twist of meaning, this collective inferiority bestowed further value upon the local-organizational "us." The Israeli identity, in other words, was founded on two distinct themes—a character type and a shared marginality—and both of these themes were the building blocks of members' sense of superiority and worth inside the united Globalint.

As far as the first theme—a character type—was concerned, the notion of a pre-existing personality template both essentialized and polarized difference between the Israelis and Americans of Globalint. In correspondence to the findings of Part I, national identity became a powerful means with which to anchor the local-organizational boundary, especially once the Jewish identity was excluded from the realm of legitimate discourse and rendered gossip. "People," Anthony Cohen (1985: 117) claims, "can 'think themselves into difference,'" making "virtually anything grist to the symbolic mill of cultural distance." Schedules, hierarchies, goals, role commitments, status titles, traveling habits—seemingly every possible aspect of organizational life indeed became "grist," forced into the blueprint of stereotypical national polarity which, in turn, granted these endless marks of organizational difference the status of "natural," pre-existing facts. In other words, the social construction of one identity—the local-organizational "us"—was both solidified and camouflaged by the construction of another—the Israeli "us"; by the fact that members defined themselves as being shaped by "natural," inevitable national forces outside of their individual selves and the organization.

So, one might ask, do Israelis "really" carry around a collective essence? Are they "really" collectivist or egalitarian, as cross-cultural writers (see Hofstede 1980; 1991; 2001) depict them? The analysis presented here implies that this depiction must be tackled with the possibility that many Israelis simply like to see themselves that way; that in everyday life and probably also in supposedly objective research questionnaires the people themselves reproduce such assumptions as positive stereotypes, continually recreating them rather than being passively determined by them. Indeed, cast in this light, cross-cultural writers themselves may be seen as bolstering, however unwittingly, the national dichotomies, bestowing upon the "symbolic mill of cultural distance" the stamp of scientific truth. Conceptualizing national identity in terms of a predetermined, collective essence, cross-cultural writers not only overlook the space of choice members have in constructing national identity, but also reify and objectify such constructs as scientifically "real" (Ailon, forthcoming; in this regard see also Jack & Lorbiecki 2003).

Within Isrocom, the construction of Israeli identity as a predetermined personality entailed a paradoxical effect. Using it to both solidify boundaries and aggrandize worth, members assembled a seemingly endless array of polarized national oppositions. This talk of difference, however, was actually based more on what they had in common with their American others than on what they did not (see Barth 1969). Namely, while the national personality templates may have been defined as contrasting, the world of meaning that had rendered them a contrast and made them comparable was one: the world of organizational instrumentality in which the values of time discipline, personal dedication, work diligence, efficiency, goal commitment, and so forth are treated as taken-for-granted truths. In their national distinctions, members sanctified these values and, moreover, embraced them as an integral part of the Israeli manifestation of organizational membership. This way, the very attempt to construct distinctiveness paradoxically wore away that distinctiveness, turning it into one of form, not content. Every overt expression of difference, in short, was actually based upon the silent embrace of an underlying commonality.

Moreover, the underlying commonality—the ideals of the corporate world—are to a large extent American. Homi Bhabha's (1990: 4) claim that "The 'other' is never outside or beyond us" thus seems especially true here. While Isrocom's members redirected the meanings of such American ideals, wresting them from the merger partners and turning them to their advantage, in so doing they were also reaffirming the superiority of an ethos that was as American as their organizational others. This, however, did not seem problematic for them. On the contrary, not only did members acknowledge American superiority, they also celebrated it, perceiving it as a factor that aggrandized their own organizational status. For them, the general superiority of America on the outside bolstered the status of the non-Americans on the inside, their accomplishments made ever more impressive by the fact that they had beaten Americans on their own ideological turf.[12]

Yet this victory of sorts should not obscure the fact of an entailed price. The specific superiority of the local-organizational identity of Isrocom's members was conditioned upon the acceptance of the general subordination of the Israeli identity; upon the affirmation of a scheme of global hierarchy that renders it inferior and marginalized. Thus, as members of Isrocom paradoxically claimed that their Israeliness had made them the "true" Americans of the merged organization, they surrendered the external status of their national identity for the sake of internal status. This discursive exchange implied that, at least within Isrocom, the Israeli identity amounted to much less than the "imagined community" that Benedict Anderson (1983) talked about. At most, it was an imagined homogeneity; a theory of common traits that constituted an unusual brand of mimicry (Bhabha 1994): not one that looks like acquiescence while slyly hiding evasive forms of resistance (the usual focus of postcolonial writers). Rather, it was one that masquerades as resistance—against America, Americans, Americanness—while slyly hiding evasive forms of acquiescence. Inside Isrocom, in short, the Israeli identity had become a mimicked Americanness surpassing its origin.

But along with all paradoxical forms of self-idealization—the claim to superior character, to defeating the undefeatable, to surpassing the origin—there was also a certain amount of self-criticism. For some, the Israeli identity was not only the source of the merit and status of the local-organizational "us," of qualities that render it internally superior, but also of its faults. The celebrated stereotype, it thus seems, also carried some negative connotations that cast a different light upon the overruling identity project and the self-idealizing efforts that it was otherwise made to serve. In other words, the symbolic building block with which the notion of a superior organizational "us" was constructed—national identity—also brought to mind flows of meaning that challenged it. Aligning the national with the local-organizational could not fix meaning: the same symbolic means that were deployed to solidify value carried overtones that undermined it as well.

Moreover, the local-organizational identity project faced other emergent challenges as well. As illustrated in Part I, in the course of everyday merger life, there were other identities—for example occupational and hierarchical—that rose to the social fore. Global in scope and thus encircling members from both merger sites, these other identities sometimes cut through the enacted local boundary. How did members make sense of them? What meanings did they attribute to them? It is to these questions that we now turn.

CHAPTER 6

Work Identities

Difference and Dilemma

"We don't have a cubicle available for you yet," said the manager to the new guy in a Scott Adams *Dilbert* cartoon, "so I'm declaring this part of the carpet to be your office." "Can I put a tape on the carpet to mark my boundary?" the new guy asks. Taking out what looks like a dog collar, the manager replies, "That won't be necessary, thanks to this hi-tech device. It will give a mild shock if you cross your invisible boundary." "The new guy hasn't left that spot for a week," a colleague reports a cartoon-box later, and Dilbert explains, "Wally taught him to beg for food." This episode, like various others, hung on a wall leading to a group of open-space cubicles in the R&D department. Though born in the United States, Dilbert and his friends were obviously at home here, too. Their occupational experiences and general condition of subordination to a high-tech organization and its agents appeared to be known to and shared by Isrocom's Israelis.

For decades, sociologists have pointed out the deep symbolic and experiential significance of work. Occupational subcultures, they claim (Van Maanen & Barley 1984; Trice 1993), offer a common normative perspective and a collective agenda that bind people together, incite solidarity, and constitute a critical axis of identification.[1] In a similar vein, writers describe shared subordination[2] as an experience that often leads to common and prominent self-definitions. Marked by a critical stance toward the organization or its agents, such co-subordination sometimes mobilizes emotion and action in ways that controvert corporate ideologies and formal versions of membership.[3]

Interestingly, as the popularity of the *Dilbert* cartoons in Isrocom indicates, both of these work-related identities—occupational and co-subordination—are generally free from the trope of locality. In contrast to the case of national identity (previous chapter), there is no apparent homology between these identities and particular terrains (see Hannerz 1996; Ben-Ari & Elron 2001). Thus, as discussed in Part I, within Globalint there were, for example, project managers or computer programmers on both merger sides, as there were many cases in which Israelis and Americans were jointly subordinated to the same manager or sources of authority. The occupational and co-subordination associations thus cut across the local-organizational boundary and, at least in potential, offered an alternative form of solidarity. How, I thus ask in this chapter, did members interpret and make sense of these global circles of attachments in the context of the continual enactment of a local one?

The answer to this question is twofold, and it will be specified in the next two sections. Briefly, the first section will show how members read difference into these global circles of identities, casting them in the mold of the split between the "us" and the "them." The second section will examine the sense of bond and attachment that endured this split, marking out an aspect of organizational life in which globalism prevailed after all.

In the Mold of the Split between the "Us" and the "Them"

Isrocom's members engaged in diverse lines of work. These may be divided into four major types: customer interface, technical, staff, and managerial work.[4] In an attempt to understand how members made sense of their shared identity with occupational colleagues from Amerotech, this section will focus on four occupations that belonged to each of these types: project managers, computer programmers, human resource workers, and managers.[5] Additionally, in its final part, the section will also examine members' perceptions of their American co-subordinates.

Project managers (marketing engineers) usually referred to their occupational line of work in terms of three major components: the client, the market, and the sale. In their accounts, they translated each into binary, oppositional categories: it was their view that with regard to each of these components national and organizational difference prevailed, demarcating them and their work style from their American colleagues. Thus, referring to the issue of clients, they repeatedly characterized their own work style as based upon a greater emphasis on direct contact with clients. "We do a lot more, we go out to the field," said a project manager, "they sit at their offices and produce nice papers and a lot of press releases; sit at their office and the world is far away." Another project manager further explains:

> There are of course differences between the way that we, the project managers, worked in legacy Isrocom and the way that they worked as project managers. There are differences. . . . Here we worked a lot with the client . . . (while) they

sat way behind in the rear, in New York. . . . I think that, as much as I understand it, the New York people see the advantage in our way of working, and they think that this notion is right, the notion that project managers should have direct contact with clients.

Similarly, another project manager expresses a similar claim when mentioning Amerotech's widespread practice of hiring subcontractors for customer contact:

> The New York way is very different than my way. They sit in their office and they administratively manage the project and there is someone else out in the field taking care of customer contact and things that happen in the field. That is not compatible with Isrocom. . . . Customer contact—how is it possible to manage a project without contact with the customer?

With regard to the second component of their line of work—the market—members claimed that they were unlike the merger partners both in terms of the ability to tune into market trends and to adopt a wide global perspective. In both respects they again asserted binary distinctions and registered critique. A senior project manager offers an example, referring to the issue of tuning into market trends. Note how his claim reproduces one of the stereotypical national distinctions (discussed in the previous chapter) to the occupational realm:

> When we identify business opportunities and we decide that they are worthwhile to us, we chase after them. This is our flexibility. (Sometimes) you chase after an opportunity without being completely equipped for the war, so-to-speak, and then you have to improvise as you go along because after you start running you find yourself in situations in which you have to somehow manage yourself. And we are used to managing ourselves this way. Okay, so we don't have all of the presentations prepared, all of the tools that marketing engineers need. So we improvise through motion, on the flight or in the morning before the meeting. . . . Generally in the United States, people are more planned. I think it is something in the core American culture. As early as when people are born they know what college they'll be going to, because their father went to that college and their grandfather went to that college. And they also plan vacations way in advance. They plan much more.

With regard to a global perspective, a project manager attributes to his American colleagues a narrow focus, reproducing yet another stereotypical national distinction to the occupational realm:

> Americans are very interested in what is going on in America and they are almost completely uninterested in what is happening outside. This is typical of them. Even their product is like that. It is very suited for the American market and it is

very ill-suited for the global market. I mean, it fits the United States and Japan like a glove to a hand, but it doesn't suit other markets very well. They ask: 'What, the European market isn't like the American market?' No! The entire world is not American. It is different!

A similar perception of difference concerned the third component of their work: sales. Yet here the moral attitude of the locals was somewhat more ambivalent, and they often declared themselves inferior in terms of sales talents, especially those related to impression management. A project manager offers an example:

> They have some marketing talents that are typical of American companies. Talents that we don't have. (Like what?) They really know how to present things both aesthetically and politically.

At the same time, however, members also attributed disadvantages to their merger partners' alleged sales style. A senior project manager illustrates:

> I see a very aggressive sales style in New York. Very aggressive, very individualistic. I mean, I see people wanting to succeed on their own, sales people from legacy New York wanting to do sales themselves, wanting to succeed by themselves, thinking that they know everything. They have contacts everywhere, they sell themselves very well. Especially themselves! (laughs) The spirit here was this: today you have to invest in a certain project, so I will help you with it. So what if you will earn the commission here? I will help you. I will run forward with you.

Thus, characterizing sales people from Amerotech as overly individualistic and driven by self-interests, the project manager constructs an opposing, idealized notion of the locals as team oriented, willing to chip in and help others make sales.

In sum, project managers spoke of their Amerotech colleagues in terms of difference. Invested in a symbolic effort to redefine local boundaries, they registered difference in terms of the basic components of their occupational work: clients, market, and sales. This way, they stretched bifurcation into the occupational realm, casting this transnational source of commonality in the mold of the overruling split. Moreover, while acknowledging the professedly American sales-talent of impression management, members generally perceived the polarized distinctions in their own normative favor, framing themselves as better in terms of accepted marketing ideals.

Computer programmers, the second occupational group, referred to three major components of their work: the programming mind, the programming work process, and the product. With regard to each, their orientation toward the merger partners was similar to that of the project managers: each component was represented in terms of a national and organizational contrast. Referring to the programming mind, a computer programmer thus says:

> Israelis improvise and Americans don't know how to do this. . . . They think very, very squarely. If a client asks for something then they will do it like he says. Israelis say: let's think, maybe it is possible to do it differently. Eventually the client will get what he wants, maybe even something better, let's explain this to him, let's think differently. It is very difficult for them to think like this.

The construction of Americans as "square" or conceptually rigid was expressed through a variety of other related typifications: "they cannot do many things simultaneously," said, for example, another programmer, "they are not spontaneous, their mind is inflexible sometimes." And another further added: "they are clerk-like, working within the confines of well-defined work areas, each one responsible for a bounded role and nothing beyond it."

Interestingly, however, when the other occupational components were referred to—the programming work process and product—the contrast was reversed. If, in relation to the programming mind, members described themselves as flexible, creative, spontaneous, and unbounded, then in relation to the work process and product they defined themselves as more ordered, cautious, thoroughly detailed, and tightly disciplined. A computer programmer offers an example that concerns the local work method:

> The impression I got, and not just from one incident but from a few incidents, is that the guys over there have a tendency to develop blindly. I mean, they have a tendency to proceed very quickly toward a certain target without market survey or benchmarks or complex analyses. It seems that their successes were, at least in some cases, out of luck. In contrast with what is happening here. I mean, we are almost at the other extreme. We work slowly, carefully, with a lot of design documents and discussions.

Another programmer poses planning and discipline as distinguishing ideals that privilege the local side, this time referring not to the work process but to the product:

> They do things quickly without too much planning. It has a cost. In order to maintain their system they have a fleet of six hundred people that do development for all kinds of customers. We settle for about a third. They have a mess. There isn't really one product. There are a lot of software versions. It looks like a monster with many heads, each one running in a different direction. In Net we always tried to link everything into a single unitary product, to drain all of the projects into it.

Thus, the notion of Americans' methodic planning—cited in the previous chapter—was abandoned when occupational values rendered it problematic for the locals. Shuttling between the binary poles of the planning-ability dichotomy, members who referred to the issues of work process and product dropped the obsessive-planning typification from the stereotypical package otherwise attributed to Americans and claimed it for themselves. These reverse-citations, it seems, highlight the fact that it is not the content of the distinction that is fixed here (there apparently isn't any absolute planning quality that can be used to distinguish either side) but its dichotomous form; not the content of the split but the fact of the splitting. As such, these citations also bring to light the gap between the decisiveness with which such distinctions were asserted and the flexibility of the content that was cast in their mold.

While generally engaged in the effort to construct superior self-worth, local computer programmers nevertheless admitted inferiority in one sense: the technical instruments that were put to use in their product. Here, the polarized sense of difference was referred to in terms that privilege the merger partners. For example:

> Their current system is in some aspects better. . . . I have a feeling that they are ahead of us in some aspects. They have things that we (only) thought about. Their hardware is ahead of Net. They have a graphic instrument that we wanted. We wanted it and they've already got it.

In sum, local computer programmers cast the joint occupation in the mold of a split between two locally defined "types." The split concerned difference in the programming mind, work process, and product. With regard to the former, members asserted themselves superior in the sense of being more flexible, inclined to improvise, and open-minded than the merger partners, and with regard to the latter two they asserted themselves superior in the sense of being rigidly disciplined, formal, and detail-oriented. When referring to the product, however, members also admitted their own side's inferiority in relation to the technical instruments that were implemented by their colleagues.

Human resource (HR) workers, another of Isrocom's occupational groups, also postulated work-related dichotomies. Specifically, they constructed occupational boundaries with regard to the balancing of HR's twin (and largely oxymoronic) commitments to both management and workers. Generally, HR personnel claimed that their merger partners—in contrast to them—have been wrongly tilting the balance toward the workers' side. An HR manager illustrates this claim:

> They are less of a business partner. I mean, as an HR manager my professional perception is that I am also a member of management and I have to produce a fragile balance between the needs of the workers and the needs of the company. To create the best possible synthesis for the company and the workers together.

Also associated with the HR-balance issue, was criticism that Amerotech's HR function took over some of the responsibilities and duties of managers and made them its own:

> There is a difference in perception between the HR in Isrocom and New York. I think that in New York they are much more involved in many more things than we are in Isrocom. I am not saying this in a positive way. I may be overly capti- vated by Isrocom's concept, but in my eyes theirs is over-involvement. I think that they are involved in places that we expect managers to be involved. Take workers' dissatisfaction as an example. Our expectation is that a worker will turn to his manager, that he will let the manager know that he is not satisfied, and the manager will take care of it. If the manager needs help or assistance or something then he can use HR. I have a feeling that over there HR rather than the manager is the first address to turn to.

Thus, the proclaimed distinguishing virtue of the local HR function con- cerned its members' acceptance of the limits of their occupational role in the division of labor with management.

Referring to HR's relationship with workers, there were two major issues that members spoke of self-critically, praising the American merger partners for achievements that they had failed to accomplish. Interestingly, these ele- ments were exactly those that members of the other occupations referred to: technical instrumentality and impression management. Since the first is linked more to material and technical resources than to occupational abili- ties, and the second more to occupational appearance or public relations than to occupational essence or substance, in both cases members seemed to channel their self-critique to sites that did not threaten their sense of oc- cupational worth: they registered criticism and defused its sting at the same time. Following is an example that concerns technical instrumentality:

> There are things that they are better at than we are and these are communica- tion channels; the instruments that they have. As a result of this advantage they had much better communications with workers over there. For example, internet, intranet, things like that. . . . In Isrocom we didn't have all of their instruments and the issue of communicating information was much more dependent upon the efforts of managers, upon what every manager did in order to ensure that workers will get the relevant information. The managers didn't always remember things, they didn't always do this well enough.

Thus, in this example an admitted weakness of the local HR function is blamed upon insufficient technological instruments and uncooperative managers. The American HR function is praised not for its people but for its machines. Similarly, in the next citation it is praised not for its substan- tive contribution but for its impression management:

The HR's role over there . . . they invest a lot of energy in "*how* to communicate" to workers. This is important. They do it much better than we do it: public relations to the workers.

Other worker-related HR duties were discussed with a clear-cut normative preference toward local ways. An HR worker offers an example that concerns commitment and availability:

Even though we are not very organized we simply do more. We deliver. We are always swamped with people who turn to us. When we visited them, for hours we didn't see a single person knocking on a door, and here the hallway is always full of people. We did not spot over there the dynamics of an open dialogue in the physical sense. They don't have cellular phones, we have them all the time. When I come in to work I immediately listen to messages and do so continually until I get home.

Another HR manager speaks of the issue of wages, framing Amerotech's approach as overly bureaucratic. Note, once again, how flexible symbols can be: the HR manager in this citation equates the attitude of Amerotech's HR to a very local Israeli institution, the *Histadrut*. This is the Israeli national labor union, a local symbol of bureaucratic vices such as inefficiency, extensive rigidity, and procedural rather than service orientation:

They have a different world view concerning wages. Here there is a higher differentiation. Over there you are categorized into a formal box and it has a wage range. It is more bureaucratic. . . . A little like the *Histadrut's* ranks, excuse me for saying this, but this is my connotation. Here, if a person is better, he gets more money. It doesn't matter what his title is. Or, if a person moves from one title to another it doesn't automatically imply a raise. Over there, if you move from one title to another then, boom! It affects your salary.

Extreme bureaucratization was also referred to with regard to other HR responsibilities. An HR worker explains:

It surprised me in the beginning because all of the organizational theories originate from the United States, theories of motivation, work incentives, leadership etc. And what I found there was something procedural. Everything is about what the law requires. . . . That is what I found in New York. It was a surprise for me. Since I did not merge with a hundred companies I tried to find out if this is typical of American companies in general. Well, it isn't necessarily typical. It seems to be something that is characteristic of New York.

Note in this citation how an explicit distinction is made between Amerotech and other American companies. This decoupling enables both to assert the latter as an occupational ideal and to ascribe to the former a low occupational status.

Thus, in the case of human resources the boundaries that, in the locals' accounts, distinguished them from their merger partners concerned two major occupational duties: those related to management and those related to workers. With respect to most issues, members praised their local occupational group's work methods. The exceptions were issues pertaining to occupational instruments and appearance.

Managers, the fourth occupational group, also presented both of these elements—occupational instruments and appearance—as an American advantage. Again registering self-criticism and defusing (if not contradicting) it at the same time, they deemed these advantages a superior wrapping of an inferior substance. A senior manager illustrates:

> The thing that is characteristic of them is that they put a lot of effort into the aesthetics of paperwork. Take their presentations as an example. They are really professional, a pleasure to look at. But when you search beyond it—there is no proportion between what they prepare and what they know. Over here we don't know how to prepare a presentation. We should learn from them in this regard. Over here everything is sloppy, slides are poor. (But) their presentations conceal a large void.

Some Israeli managers animated this claim with narratives of the early merger days: they recalled how Amerotech's managers had impressed them in the beginning and described the feelings of inferiority and unworthiness that this impression created. Then they spoke of a revelation of truth in which they had come to realize that their colleagues were better than them in managing appearances, not organizations. A member of middle management illustrates this distinctive plot:

> In the initial stages of the merger we experienced some feelings of inferiority. . . . The data that they reported, their slides, their presentations, everything was presented as ideal. We were really defensive during the first several day, feeling a need to understand how come we are what we are and they are so good. . . . They arrived here looking like a really integrated team. They made a great impression in the first several days. A management team from the movies. Legendary. Excellent cooperation, everyone is a professional in his field. Really, they were something. But slowly, from slide to slide, we began to realize that there are gaps between the way that they appeared and the true situation. . . . Slowly it became clear that we were the ones who had made the right decisions. There was some uncertainty in the beginning but the truth slowly revealed itself.

Some local managers denounced their colleagues' occupational capabilities not only in relation to the way that they presented themselves in the initial merger days, but also in relation to the information that they routinely presented to decision makers. In their account, these managers repeatedly portrayed their American colleagues as managers who reduce their role to the superficial task of presenting general impressions to those on top, ridding themselves of substantive responsibility for understanding and managing details. Illustrating this dichotomous generalization, a manager devalues the occupational expertise of his American colleagues:

> The American manager is much less detail oriented. The Israeli manager knows how to get down to details. How to tell the worker, 'Prove what you are saying. I want to know the details. I want to know why you are saying that it is like this when I know something else.' To dive in, to get down to details. The American is not like that. The American receives data, processes it, and presents it. He is very detached. He does not dive in through motion, he doesn't think, he doesn't brainstorm. He is given data, he takes it, he organizes it, he rearranges it, he presents it. The criticizers say that a lot of it is garbage in, garbage out.

Related to this distinction was another that concerned managers' relative power within the system. A manager explains:

> The orderly American method with its procedures is very dangerous for managers because they don't have power. Their power isn't substantial. It is impossible to learn what is going on from reports and paperwork and monthly discussions. What happens is, that the managers over there are very detached from everyday life and in practice they don't manage the company. Rather, the company manages them. . . . An Israeli manager over here really knows what is going on, he can really affect things, manage things. Tom, for example, can't.

Two other oft-cited distinctions between Israeli and American managers concerned flexibility and efficiency. A senior manager describes Israeli managers as more flexible, again demonstrating the reproduction of a stereotypical national distinction to this particular occupational universe:

> Israelis have a wider perspective, an ability to improvise, and higher flexibility. These are the basic abilities with which we run the business. Isrocom is for me an opportunistic company. . . . There is flexibility to come and say, wait a minute, we are identifying a trend. We won't say, 'wait a minute, let's put it into the planning procedure,' because then it'll take us another year to move ourselves . . . the Americans, however, are more planned.

Concerning efficiency, local managers spoke of both money and labor. Thus claims a manager with regard to money:

> A thing that was typical of them is that they did not monitor expenses. They were very wasteful. The wallet was open. When you analyze results you find that while they had similar sales scopes they hardly earned anything in comparison to Isrocom. For example, everyone flew business class, every secretary, every clerk. Over here everyone—from the CEO to the last of the engineers—everyone flew coach.

And thus claims another manager with regard to the management of labor:

> With the right management it is possible to accomplish much more than what they accomplished and with less personnel. This is culture, there is nothing you can do about it. They worked in a different way. We know how to extract 200% out of our people. They extract maybe 25% out of theirs.

In sum, the local managers asserted four major occupational contrasts: impression versus detail management, narrow versus wide involvement, rigidity versus flexibility, and wastefulness versus efficiency. This occupational package of distinctions, clearly resonating with the organizational "us" versus "them" dichotomy, was generally used for self-aggrandizement. The local managers framed themselves as occupationally superior in all but the somewhat ambivalent issues of technical instrumentality and impression management.

Thus, in the cases of project managers, computer programmers, HR workers, and managers, Isrocom's members subjected occupational attachments to the overruling discourse of difference. In their accounts, distinctions of national and organizational origin left a mark upon these global identities, manifesting themselves in the discrete achievements, talents, and orientations that were characteristic of people from each side. As bifurcation was thus applied to many fields of activity at once, a seemingly endless array of "examples" were attached to it, augmenting its persuasive effect and making it seem natural and fixed. Moreover, with regard to most of these "examples," members talked of their own occupational type as a better or superior manifestation of valued ideals, though interestingly these ideals diverged from one global identity to the other, and, as the computer programmers illustrated, even within them. The exceptions were technical instrumentality and impression management skills, both repeatedly attributed to the merger partners, rendering them well equipped and well presented but otherwise inferior. The stereotypical trait-based split between the "us" and the "them," in short, was generally reproduced within diverse spheres of global attachments.

Moreover, as claimed in the beginning of the chapter, members shared another form of affiliation across the Isrocom/Amerotech divide besides the one related to their occupations: **co-subordination**. In other words, regardless of the type of work they performed, the locals also had hierarchically defined associations with members from abroad who were subjected to the same sources of authority. These associations potentially offered an alternative form of solidarity. Interestingly, however, they too were cast in a mold of a split. When referring to co-subordinates from Amerotech, Isrocom's members marked a boundary of difference in relation to the issue of deference toward managers. Local subordinates, they claimed, perceive and treat managers more as their equals than as their superiors, never letting subordination monitor their thoughts or actions; never internalizing the notion that they are of lesser abilities or rights than those on top. A project manager thus says:

> Our president always says that in the company every one of the workers thinks that he can do the work of the president or the CEO at least as good as they can, if not better, but at least as good. . . . There are a lot of people who walk around here saying, 'So the president said this, so what? He is wrong—we're very sorry, but it is the president who has a problem . . . ' Here a manager is seen as just another person. He is the manager, so what? Over there if a manager says X, then X is what it will be.

A system engineer augments the persuasive effect of this polarized generalization with a joke:

> There is a nice joke that illustrates what I want to say: Once when Roosevelt and Weitzman (the first President of Israel) met, Roosevelt told Weitzman, 'Oh, it must be easy for you. You only have 2 million citizens. I have 200 million.' So Weitzman answered Roosevelt, 'Mr. President you are mistaken. You have 200 million citizens; I have 2 million presidents.' This joke is right to the point. I mean, I saw this in our meeting with them. For New York's engineers whenever a manager says something everyone immediately follows in his track. But in Israel whatever a manager says is at best a recommendation. I mean, anyone can say anything he likes, no one has to follow the track that was set by a manager. We will speak out our opinions, we will say what we think is best.

A computer programmer makes a similar point, framing a specific event as an illustration of a general type:

> If a certain superior says a sentence in the States it is sacred. Here it isn't like this at all (laughs). In our meetings with Jim, whenever Yiftah (a manager) said something, it doesn't matter what, even if it was opposed to Jim's opinion, then that was it. Jim accepted it. I think this is just polite politeness.

Thus, when members referred to co-subordinates from Amerotech they constructed two antithetical "bad" and "good" orientations to subordination: a negative one that sanctifies submission and a positive one that refuses to do so. In their accounts, they attributed the former to their merger partners and the latter to themselves. This way, co-subordination discourse, too, had turned into a means for enhancing the image of the organizational universe as divided into two absolutely and irreconcilably different parts and, furthermore, for enhancing the status of the locals within it.

And yet some aspects of the occupational and co-subordination attachments did, nevertheless, endure. Despite the fact that the occupational and co-subordination identities were so thoroughly cast in the mold of the split, and despite the obvious attempt to fix polarity and secure symbolic closure in representing the boundaries between the "us" and the "them," some space remained for globalism after all.

Bonds Despite Difference

In a joint customer support training that was held in Amsterdam, a handful of Israelis were excused from a workshop session that they had all taken before. Having several free hours at their disposal and a video camera that one of them brought to the trip, they undertook the task of creating a humorous film about the life of customer support engineers. The event's organizers requested that they would be politically correct and careful so as not to offend their American merger partners. Nevertheless, the Israelis had their minds set on creating an uncensured film. "It seemed to me," one of them said, "that they were blowing things completely out of proportion. We left in all of the scenes despite their warnings." Moreover, refusing to adhere to these managerial rules of performance and seeking to convey their perceptions without restriction, the engineers opened the film with a cynical climax. The first scene, "A Team Leader is Born," shows a nurse and a doctor with improvised medical outfits accepting the (pillow-) pregnant and moaning Mrs. Customer Support for delivery. After helping her lie down on a (hotel) bed and covering her with a sheet, they shout, "Push! Push!" Finally, a diapered man emerges from under the covers, sucking on the antenna of a cellular phone.

The remaining scenes deal with adulthood. The second scene is about a hysterical client who calls the "Customer Support Hotline" which, in the third scene, turns out to be an indifferent man sitting comfortably on a terrace facing the ocean, asking for details, which he does not even bother to write down. The fourth and fifth scenes are both bedroom scenes, depicting two variants of customer support engineers' married life. In the fourth scene the wife of an engineer with an "On Call Engineer" sign hanging above his sleeping head answers a client's call in the middle of the night. After failing to wake up her tired husband, she tells the caller, "You should do reset!," hangs up, and goes back to sleep. In the next scene both the husband and the wife are engineers, and when the phone rings and wakes them they pass it back and forth, each assuring the other that the problem concerns his or her field of expertise.

Finally, the last two scenes depict work meetings. The first of them is run by an American manager. Talking on the phone with a Japanese client, he (literally) bows down and agrees to every single one of the client's requests. The second meeting is headed by a sloppy, lazy, and unprofessional caricature of an Israeli manager. These last two scenes, it should be noted, are the only ones explicitly dealing with the Israeli/American split. However, they do so in a way that actually reshuffles the hierarchy of identities. By attributing the national split solely to managers, and by caricaturing and ridiculing it, these scenes do not allow nationality to dominate the discourse of identity and use it instead to accentuate a different set of transnational "us"s: subordinates, colleagues, audience. The group of engineers thus designed an uncensored, humorous, and cynical representation of their conceptions of their work and managers; of their occupational and co-subordination identities.

After the film was completed, it was presented at the closing session of the training. Interestingly, during the time that it was projected its creators purposely posed their video camera in front of the audience, filming its response. Thus, not only did they insist upon articulating their identity perception to the (partly) American audience in an uncensored way, but they were also curious to discover whether or not their audience identified with it. They were examining the boundaries between the Isrocom and Amerotech parts of their global identity group, testing their existence, checking their significance. Their "findings" indicated that the social boundaries that set the locals from their counterparts were at least in some ways permeable. "They liked the film, they laughed and smiled," one of them told me, and another said, "They got most of the jokes. They didn't laugh at all of them but they did laugh at most of them." Indeed, judging by what was filmed, the Israeli-American audience seemed quite homogenous: a joint body of people silently watching a scene, then laughing at the punch line, and finally clapping enthusiastically in a unified way. Enough seemed to be in common to challenge all that was not.

Boundaries, Bridges, and Moral Hazards

The tendency to view identities in ways that transcend the mold of the binary split was apparent not only in the customer-support engineers' film, but also in somewhat less artistic and more realistic narratives that members produced in the course of interviews. These narratives were accounts of particular relationships with colleagues from Amerotech; stories not of the generalized and stereotyped "us" and "them" but of a specific "me" and "her/him." Such narrated accounts were very rare in comparison to the widespread talk of distinctions and reserved to those who had a chance to become actively engaged in such a work-relationship. And still, taken seriously, these accounts are a testament of the meaningful role of occupational and co-subordination ties in inspiring, giving shape to, and constituting the language of global bonds and attachments.

As examples, I will present here three such narratives. The narratives are ordered in an ascending order: in the first, Ziv's tale, a global bond is recognized but eventually rejected. In the second, Haim's tale, the global bond is stronger and there is an actual attempt of accommodation. In the third, Ilan's tale, the global bond is embraced and presented as an overruling source of commitment.

Ziv, a hardware engineer, had at the time of the merger been working in Isrocom for over seven years. Recalling his career in the organization, he explained that he had heard of the company during his military service, remembered it during his studies for a degree in engineering, chose it as his first workplace, and stayed ever since. "I came because I heard about the system that was being developed here and it sounded interesting to me," he explained the professional incentive of his decision to join the company. When work on Net2, the revolutionary product that was originally destined to replace Net, began, he was one of the first to take part in it. After almost five years of work in the company, he attested to being "pretty much of an expert in my field," and thus suitable to pioneer such a pretentious, futuristic project.

Immediately after the merger, two senior engineers from Amerotech came for meetings in Tel Aviv to discuss Globalint's future product plan. "We bonded very well, very openly, very professionally," Ziv summarized those first meetings. Nonetheless, the initial professional bonding was soon overshadowed by contention about the design of the future product, with each side promoting its own product perception and past work. "It was a great struggle," Ziv maintained. Management, as it turned out, preferred New York's product strategy for various business reasons (see Chapter 2), and this was, Ziv declared, "a pretty big shock." Consequently, he claimed, the local engineers tried to save as much as possible of their work. "Nobody likes to be told that what you have been working on is no longer needed," Ziv explained. "So at a certain stage we sat down together and it became obvious to us that we have a mission: to show that the other side's theory is impracticable, that there is no choice but to preserve what we have been doing. . . . That it is impossible to modify our product in their way and, thus, that it is necessary to maintain our work."

However, Ziv's commitment to this mission was, according to his tale, morally shaded by the identity that he shared with the American merger partners. "It really disturbed me personally," he said, "to be engaged in such *negative*-engineering. We were not trying to see how something *can* be done. We were trying to prove why their solution was impossible." Thus, his commitment to the local group came into a disturbing conflict with his engineering identity, its values and perceptions of right and wrong. Ziv's tale, in other words, now reached a drama of identity, one that concerned the making of a choice between what were presented as commitments of equivalent weights. The solution to Ziv's conflict involved a they-did-it-first kind of justification: the merger partners, he basically claimed, were the ones who originally

defied the moral relevance of the global engineering identity to the definition of the situation. "The explanation that I gave to myself, and I think that
it is true," he said, rescuing his sense of virtue and creating himself in narrative as harboring uncompromised commitments, "was that the other side
did not play fairly. The other side denied things that were fundamental and
substantial elements of fair play. The other side, New York, and the manager
over there, James Clark—he complained about us to management and there
were other such manifestations of un-colleagual behavior. At least that's how
it looked from our side. We asked him for information. . . . He said, 'Yes,
yes, sure,' but it never arrived." Thus, though eventually rejected, the global
engineering identity did set some moral claims that reportedly affected Ziv's
thoughts and actions. No longer discursively suppressed and in fact narratively brought to the same level as his local commitment, it pressed him to
seek justification for his local agency.

Moreover, not all such tales of dilemma ended this way. **Haim,** a technical
writer, told me a story about how he actually sought to fulfill his conflicting,
local and global dues. His sense of commitment to colleagues from Amerotech was inspired, he said, in a meeting in which they confronted him with
the claim that the merger was a collectively sustained disguise of an Israeli
takeover. "I had a meeting in New York with two of my colleagues, Don and
Alice, and their subcontractor was also present," he recalled. "We discussed
a professional matter. All of a sudden I heard the word 'takeover.' Don said
'takeover.' I was completely shocked. This was the first time that I had ever
heard that word from someone in New York. I've heard it here before, but
not over there." Don and Alice, he further told me, spoke to him not only as
a member of the taking-over side, but also as a co-subordinate. "Both Don
and Alice were low level workers, my level workers," he said in an empathic
tone, posing this fact as the interpretive axis of his tale. "They were what I
call 'A-Zero': I once had an argument with an Assistant Vice President and
I felt that I was coming on too strong, so I told him, 'Listen, I'll do whatever you want because you are an Assistant Vice President and I am just a
zero.' The Assistant Vice President corrected me and said, 'Assistant Zero.'"
Laughing at this, Haim went on: "So, they are like me: Assistant Zeros."

Thus, Haim framed the interaction with Don and Alice in terms of two
incongruent identities. Wandering off to the "Assistant Zero" subnarrative as
a means for emphasizing this aspect and bringing it to the center of attention, he constructed the interpretive setup of his story: the two colleagues
addressed him as both a member of Isrocom and a co-subordinate. To them,
he was both a "them" and an "us." Returning to the original story line, he
continued: "So anyway," he said, "we talked about the things that happened
since the merger and Don spoke of it as a takeover." Haim's first reported
reaction to his colleagues' complaint was to deny it, choosing to defend his

local side and the front of a merger (rather than a takeover) that it allegedly sought to maintain. "I just stopped talking about the professional matter," he dramatically reported, "and I said, 'This is the first time that I hear that word, takeover. Up to now I heard that it is a merger.' I lied, because I heard that word over here. I heard it here, I heard the word takeover."

Nonetheless, despite the lie, Haim assured me, he was still willing and wanting to listen. "Don answered me, 'It isn't just a takeover, it's a hostile takeover.' So I told him, 'Let's forget about work, let's talk about this.'" Taking him up on his offer, Don began to explicate the difficulties that other subordinates in Amerotech had encountered. "He explained to me," Haim reported, "that 30% of the employees had already left; that they are not bringing in new people to replace them; that the corporate mood is like in *Titanic:* so many have left that they stopped throwing good-bye parties. People who've been working for four years in the company just disappeared. He said that management is trying to calm them down without actually doing anything. They don't believe management," Haim continued. "And he also told me about a destiny date: January 15th, the day that the merger will be a year and a day old. In New York's contract it says that Com will have to pay damages to workers who leave the company within the first year of the merger. This is something that is unheard of in the United States. It is a virtual destiny date, it is in their minds, and it implies that we, the Israelis, are the conquerors. . . . The Israelis who did the hostile takeover are waiting for January 15th to terminate them."

This talk about the Israeli side, Haim declared, led him to discomfort. "I could see that he was almost crying, that he was yelling, that it was difficult for him. He was in distress. I felt really uncomfortable," he said. Reportedly seeking a way out of this uncomfortable situation, he adopted an interesting path of action. He did not choose the local commitment over the global one as Ziv claimed to have done, but a combination of them both: according to his account, he acted in a way that fulfilled his duties to both the co-"A-Zeros" and the local-organizational side. "I told him that I am listening to what he is saying," Haim claimed, "and that I will talk about it with people here. I said, maybe they don't know what is going on at the level of A-Zero. Maybe the Executive VPs over here only get updates from the Executive VPs over there, and maybe they are thinking that everything is okay. So I took it upon myself to report this here." Thus, here too, in similarity to Ziv's narrative, the local and the global commitments were portrayed as laying equally forceful claims upon the narrator, leading to a dramatic conflict that demanded a careful balancing act; a careful walk on a thin identity-line.

"When I returned," Haim's narrative was now in its final chapter, "I asked for a meeting with the VP of Human Resources. I explained the situation to her. I told her: 'This is the truth.' I asked her if she feels comfortable with the way that they feel. I asked her, why won't you lengthen that contract or something?

It is just symbolic. It doesn't cost anything, and it'll calm them down. . . . I simply came to tell her what my impression was and to give a little suggestion. I did this because I thought that maybe they don't hear these things at their levels. I wanted to report that this is what's going on at the lower levels."

Haim was not very successful. "She said thank you," he described his impact upon the local side, "and the meeting was over in five minutes." However, this fact did not shade the underlying moral of his tale. Identity-wise, he came out of the entire affair morally intact: a loyal co-subordinate and a loyal member of the local side at the same time. His story, in short, was not about making a difference as much as about finding a way to pay both of his conflicting and, so it was framed, equally pressing dues.

During my stay in Isrocom I also encountered a case in which the global bonds seemed to have had an even greater effect than in the one reported by Haim. This was the story of **Ilan**, an industrial engineer with a middle management position in Operations. "I sent one of my subordinates abroad, to do a presentation in a meeting of one of the marketing departments," he began his story about an engagement with the merger partners. Arriving at the meeting, Ilan's story continues, the subordinate was asked if the presentation would also contain information about Amerotech's Operations department, and he turned to him with this question. Ilan did not know what to answer, so he sent emails to his own managers and to Fred, a managerial colleague in Amerotech's Operations department, "in order to ask them what they think. To find out if they want to add anything or remark on the presentation." The fact that he sent the email to Fred, he explained, led to some angry reactions from people in the local Operations department. "Suddenly I got an urgent voicemail from my superior," Ilan traced out the turn of events, his tone growing excited as he spoke. "He said, 'What were you thinking sending this email to Fred?' He said that the decision not to include them in the presentation is a political matter and that it doesn't make sense to do what I did. They were really angry with me over here."

After this episode, Ilan's narrative continued, he began working on a new project. At a certain point, he ran across information that he felt should be communicated to his colleagues abroad. "I discovered," he said, "that each of our suppliers is making different sorts of accommodations for the year 2000. There is a need to be aware of this, to collect information about this." But while his occupational conscience instructed him to share his discovery with his colleagues, the previous response of his local managers had framed such sharing as a breach of a local pact. In this, Ilan's tale thus reached the same focal, commanding conflict of commitments that Haim and Ziv authored as well. In other words, rather than being suppressed by the local identity project, here too the significance of the global identity narratively rises and it is presented as equally pressing.

Moreover, as claimed, Ilan's heroically framed solution to the dilemma took neither the shape of Haim's middle way, nor Ziv's unsettling discomfort at choosing to act on behalf of the local side. Rather, Ilan decided to follow his occupational conscience. "I decided to send Fred an email about this," he said, "because I thought that it would interest him, that it would help him. This time, however, I've learned from experience and I sent the email to him alone. I did not send it to anyone here in Israel." Interestingly, his justification for this was actually quite similar to the one Ziv used when rationalizing an opposite choice: Ilan, too, spoke in terms of they-did-it-first, linking his choice to the behavior of those who shared his rejected identity. This time, however, the claim was not that his identity-others defied the identity first by failing to act in solidarity, as Ziv maintained about Amerotech's engineers, but that his identity-others—the locals—defied the identity first by demanding excessive solidarity. "From their reactions to my first email you might have thought: what a crime I've committed! What a sin I've sinned! So when the next time came, I sent an email to Fred alone." Thus, while in Ziv's tale the experience of a global bond with the merger partners led to discomfort but was eventually rejected, and while in Haim's narrative it led to action that did not breach the local commitment, in Ilan's story it led to action that defied the demands and expectations of his local-others.

In sum, the split between the "us" and the "them" did not overrule all global bonds. As Ziv, Haim, and Ilan traced out stories of dramatic dilemmas necessitating difficult and discomforting choices, they created themselves in narrative as torn between equally commanding dues toward two identity groups with distinct, even contradictory, interests, goals, and notions of right and wrong. While the solutions to these conflicts of identity differed—Ziv rejected the global bond, Haim sought a middle way, and Ilan rejected the local bond—the narrators' impulse to justify their choice is a testimony of the deep significance that occupational and co-subordination ties entailed for them and the consequent stakes involved in terms of their sense of virtue. Rather than being automatically suppressed under the mold of the "us" versus "them" split, in these cases the occupational and co-subordination ties were portrayed as laying significant claims upon members, limiting the degree to which they could turn away or disconnect themselves from their American colleagues. These global ties, then, created internal dramas in which members were forced to make identity-defining choices out of their own thus acknowledged multiplicity.

Conclusions

The fate of the global occupational and co-subordination identities was basically the same as that of the merged, global-organizational identity: that of a split. It was members' perception that national and organizational distinctions left an imprint upon these identities, demarcating two locally defined types by the ways in which members from the two merger sites lived up to a variety of valued ideals. Consequently, in their view, there were significant differences between "Amerotech's engineers" and "Isrocom's engineers," "their managers" and "our managers," "American subordinates" and "Israeli subordinates," and so forth. Furthermore, members generally framed these differences in their own normative favor, speaking of themselves as superior manifestations of the global identities. The merger partners might have been referred to as having technological and presentational advantages, as possessing better instruments and form, but they were generally described as inferior in the things that mattered: achievements, orientations, methods, and characteristics. To a large extent, then, the enactment of a separate local-organizational identity took hold not only of members' Israeli identity (previous chapter), but also of their occupational and co-subordination ties. These too were "grist to the symbolic mill of cultural distance" (Cohen 1985: 117); these too were forced into coherence with the continually enacted "us" and "them." The definitions of self that members shared with their merger partners, in short, became sites within and through which organizational and national distinctions continually echoed.

The echoing sense of difference, however, did not dissolve all sense of attachment. "Wherever they go," writes Ulf Hannerz with regard to members of transnational occupations, "they find others who will interact with them in the terms of the specialized but collectively held understandings" (1996: 107). Here, too, such interactions took place. During one such occasion, it was claimed, members sought to explore the bounds of the global commonalities both by making a cynical film of their lives as customer-support engineers, and by examining their audience's reactions to it. This way, they used a visual dialogue of sorts to re-examine and reconstruct the boundaries that set them apart from their American colleagues and peers. Apparently, their efforts indicated not only that local boundaries were potentially permeable in Globalint, but that members were actually quite curious about them, willing to examine or rethink them.

Moreover, engagement with the merger partners, it was further shown, gave rise not only to curiosity and a search for commonality but also to self-conflict. As the cases of Ziv, Haim, and Ilan illustrated, tales of such engagements posed global identities as entailing a deeply felt significance. Indeed, in these tales, notions of occupational and co-subordination right and wrong, of solidarity and commitment, had enough of a bearing upon peoples' thoughts and actions to rouse discomfort and dilemma and constrain their ability to turn away from merger partners altogether. In these dramas of identity, in other words, the global identities were no longer suppressed, were no longer grist to the mill of cultural distance, but rather represented as leading to a sense of conflicting agencies; of having to choose one's ways out of what was consequently acknowledged as parallel, if incongruent, loyalties.

Interestingly, however, the tales diverged in the way the conflicts of loyalties were resolved. In contrast to the account characteristic of academic literature on identities in global organizations,[6] for Ziv, Haim, and Ilan the choice between identities was not automatic at all: in their narratives, local and global identities did not mutually exclude one another. They involved a compromise, a choice, and they necessitated justification. As they narrated themselves through these tales, they indicated how their own sense of virtue relies upon loyalty to the "them" no less than to the "us." In this sense, it seems, the occupational and co-subordination ties constituted a cultural bridge. Bearing upon people's thought and actions, they came to mean a transnational source of moral responsibility and commitment toward those who, for most other practical purposes, were delineated as "the Americans."

CHAPTER 7

Conclusion

Merging Ourselves Apart

"You and me/ We come from different worlds," sang Hootie and the Blow-fish on the first merger day. Waiters served little sandwiches with thinly cut vegetables and fish, French pancakes filled with sweet cheese, fresh fruit, and juices. Shiny pens rested in black velvet. Cries of "Mazel Tov" were heard from the door. On the screen, workers waved and smiled, and managers promised to lead the world market. Hootie and the Blowfish went on, their song listing romantic hardships safe beneath the rosy wings of cliché: "You look at me/ You got nothing left to say/ I'm gonna pout at you until I get my way/ I won't dance, you won't sing/ I just wanna love you/ But you want to wear my ring/ Well there's nothing I can do/ I only wanna be with you/ You can call me a fool/ I only wanna be with you."

Members answered this staged romanticism, this capitalist "marriage" born not in a starry-eyed embrace under a moonlit sky, but in a managerial board-room under the bright light of global ambitions, with a counterclaim concerning who they only wanna be with. They responded to the organizational identi-ty claim laid upon them through every drumbeat, through every cry of "Mazel Tov," with cynicism, parody, and a polarized representation of "us" versus "the typical American schmucks." I called their reaction a local-organizational iden-tity project and set out to examine both its enactment in everyday life and its implications for their other definitions of self. In this concluding chapter I will review my findings and consider their implications and contributions.

*****

The merger with Amerotech, I claimed, constituted a dramatic turning point in Isrocom's history. The company had always sought global status, but until the merger had remained predominantly Israeli. With the merger completed, the work lives of many members of Isrocom were globalized to a significant degree. As the organizational structures of the two merger partners were united in various ways along with their product designs, work flows, communication technologies, and "cultures," Amerotech became an integral part of Isrocom's work processes and routines. "The Americans," as they were often referred to, became teammates, colleagues, internal customers or suppliers, managers, and subordinates. Their immediate, technologically mediated, or symbolic presence became an inseparable part of everyday life.

However, the presence of Amerotech's members, it soon became apparent, created for Isrocom's members both the impetus and means for constructing a separate and locally bounded sense of organizational attachment. As Part I of this book illustrated, during face-to-face and technologically mediated communication events members redefined their original local-organizational boundary. They marked out a social terrain as their own through exclusion of merger partners, at times utilizing global technology itself for this task, and they overshadowed definitions of a merged entity with a sense of a seemingly unalterable, natural, and objective national distinction. Furthermore, during these communication events Isrocom's members also donned a collective mask of internal unity and harmony. They talked and acted in ways that blurred distinctions between them, enacting themselves as a single social whole. In events of this sort, in short, members engaged in a collective effort to enact a separate, local, and unified organizational "us."

This enacted collective identity was also sustained through representations of Amerotech members within the local site. Constituting a discursive field in which various interests came into play, identities were represented through talk, image, and text. This realm of representation allowed flow and movement. Uninterrupted by the complicating presence or "realness" of those depicted, members were free to construct images of the merger partners in accordance with their own social and political goals; to represent identities in terms of polarity and split or to register a sense of diversity that "spoiled" any notion—global or local—of neat boundaries or elegant unity. Thus, as the absent American merger partners were symbolically brought into the local context, processes of identity construction were continually fueled, albeit in a way that was ironically both more susceptible to being taken to a polarized extreme and more vulnerable to fragmentation.

Though prevalent and ongoing, the construction of a separate local-organizational identity did not completely repudiate the global version of identity that was introduced by the very act of a merger. On the contrary, the relationship between these two versions seemed one of mutual inclusion rather than mutual exclusion. As was most strikingly evident in interactions unfolding in the absence of the merger partners, the enactment of the local-organizational identity demanded that the global option be expressed and thus acknowledged in order to be contradicted. Furthermore, not only did the local identity project presuppose the global as its starting point, it also did not transgress or entirely undermine it. Indeed, even in face-to-face interactions with merger partners, when collective mobilization to create and support boundaries and to maintain a local, collective "public face" seemed at its peak, members did not refrain from passing information to or coordinating work processes with these partners. Nor did they explicitly challenge the global ambitions of the organization. The construction processes thus always unfolded within some broad overall constraints, never going so far as to undermine the foundations of the global corporation, and, at least implicitly, the global identity associated with it.

Furthermore, not only did the construction of the "us" and the "them" uphold the possibility of global unity, it also always left room for the segmentation of the local unity. Members' multiple identities were the foundation of this ever-present potential. Thus, during global communication events some non-organizational, global identities and related flows of meaning surfaced, cutting across the sustained local boundary that demarcated members of the "us" from members of the "them." In between communication events, when Isrocom's members were talking not *to* but *about* their merger partners, the local-organizational identity lost some of its vitality as the collective mask of unity and harmony was removed to reveal differentiation and diversity. Isrocom's members, in short, constructed a distinct and separate "us," but this "us" was vulnerable to being fractured by the process of construction itself; by the way it both fed upon and contradicted circles of belonging that cut through local boundaries.

Nevertheless, although partial and self-contradictory, the construction of a separate organizational identity did bear upon other identities that rose to the social fore. Part II examined national and work identities in this regard. Regarding the former, it argued that the ways members talked about the Israeli identity implied that for them it came to mean a homogenous template of an involved, dedicated, unconstrained, boundaryless personality; a stereotypical character that distinguished them from the merger partners and generally marked their greater fit with organizational ideals. Ironically, however, these organizational ideals are to a large extent of American origin. Thus, as members spoke of an Israeli cluster of traits, they also implicitly, if unintentionally, sanctified "Americanness" and positioned themselves as the "true" Americans of the merged corporation. Moreover, not only did they claim status by virtue of being "true" Americans, but also by virtue of defeating the Americans at their own game through the act of acquisition. It is through this ironic constellation of meaning that the sense of general Israeli inferiority in relation to America was celebrated as something that bolstered the collective self-image of Isrocom's members. Within Isrocom, in other words, embracing the Israeli identity as a sign of organizational virtue challenged the superiority of specific Americans, not of the general America.

The construction of a locally bounded organizational identity also left an imprint on members' work identities. In their accounts, members cast occupational and co-subordination attachments in the mold of the split between the "us" and the "them." It was their perception that the Israeli personality template and the notion of a distinct, local-organizational entity rendered the occupational colleagues and co-subordinates from Amerotech different in terms of a variety of elements and valued ideals. Moreover, with the ambivalent exceptions of impression management and instrumentality, members rendered these colleagues and peers not only different but also lesser in divergent ways that ranged from one global identity to the other. Members, in short, aligned their multiple selves, forging congruence between their ongoing local-organizational identity project on one hand, and the Israeli and work identities on the other.

Yet again complexity and incompleteness prevailed. Members did, indeed, deem the Israeli identity the constituting personality-template of the local-organizational "us," otherwise basically hollowing it out of locally distinctive normative content. But, at the same time, this identity also seemed to inspire in them some rare but significant criticism toward that "us"; to enable a somewhat distanced judgment of it to form along the contours of a discourse of faults. Similarly, while members discursively sliced occupational and co-subordination attachments in two, splitting them into locally defined types, enough sense of commonality endured to inspire curiosity and even create trans-Atlantic pressures toward loyalty to American peers. Thus, national and work identities were made to serve the local-organizational identity project, but not so much as to completely wither away or make personal identity choices automatic.

We have, then, quite an intricate process of identity formation. Isrocom's members, it seems, were engaged in two related struggles. On one hand, they resisted globalization, continuing to present themselves as distinct and worthy 'locals.' On the other hand, they embraced globalization as if it were exclusively their own, posing themselves as a purer and better manifestation of it and thus seizing the global "good" to themselves. The simultaneity of these struggles led to stereotypification and normative erosion of that which members saw as the origin of their local distinctiveness—their national identity—and to the taken-for-granted sanctification of global, capitalist values and ideals. As members defined themselves in terms of traits and achievements, in terms of being more or less equipped to pursue corporate goals and purposes, the "supermarket of identities," as it has been called (see Mathews 2000) became, at best, that of means, not ends; of form, not substance. Furthermore, the two struggles also had an impact upon central work identities that transcended the split between the locals and the outsiders, the "us" and the "them." This led to personal dilemmas; to dramatically narrated internal conflicts of having to choose one's self and one's ways out of a set of incongruent identities and related notions of right and wrong. The struggle to preserve a local sense of an organizational self, in short, eroded the meaning of "local" and made it clear that there was no single self to preserve but many to compromise.

Throughout this study, I have outlined the implications of these findings for organizational theory. These implications relate to each of the major identities that were studied—organizational, national, and work identities—and to the interrelations between them. With regard to the first, the way members went about defining and enacting organizational identity points to the limits of formal power in defining and shaping it. Although management might control some potent mediums of representation and set constraints, it is not the single and exclusive purveyor of this identity. Members too, it is clear, have the ability, the space, and the occasion to define the boundaries and meanings of their organizational belonging. A full account of organizational identity must therefore take their agency into consideration. Moreover, managerial power may itself become a means for this agency, turning against the formal version of organizational identity as managers are included, and take part in construction processes that counteract it. Theories that claim to explain the link between the formal organizational identity and members' cognitive belief systems—the general focus of mainstream research on the topic—must thus recognize the existence of creative, unpredictable, and spontaneous social processes which problematize this link by creating endless possibilities for negotiating, challenging, recreating, or altering it. Indeed, recognition of this aspect of organizational identity formation would enable organizational researchers to transcend an ongoing debate concerning the question of whether this identity is stable or malleable.[1] As the findings of this study indicate, "old," change-resistant notions of organizational identity, such as that of a local Isrocom, may be sustained in ways that are fluid and ongoing. While their form, their formal label, may seem continuous, their meanings are in a state of flux, incorporating, fracturing, and disseminating different notions and borders of groupness and attachment; different notions of what it means to belong.

The findings point to similar theoretical implications for the issue of national identity in organizations. As I suggested in the Introduction (Chapter 1), the mainstream treatment of this issue in organizational research poses national identity as a cognitive essence, one that constitutes an obstacle to the formal identities of global corporations. In contrast, the way

Israeli identity played itself out at Globalint implies that national identity, rather than a fixed a-priori essence, is to a large extent socially constructed in organizational settings, and that its relationship with the global organization is much more complex than the notion 'obstacle' seems to suggest. Here, national identity was a symbolic resource that assumed a potent role in the social production of a *sense* of difference, rather than in the psychological generation of a so-called *fact* of difference (see also Ailon-Souday & Kunda 2003). Constituting the central and standard terminology for issues of identity (Ben-Ari 1996), it was repeatedly utilized by members to sustain their sense of a bounded, local, and separate organizational "us." In the context of this symbolic appropriation of national identity to the organization realm it underwent transformations, assuming a distinct, stereotypical form albeit with global, capitalist normative content. Thus, just as the organizational identity was revealed as not completely global, national identity was revealed as not completely local, and both of these identities existed simultaneously, in some ways fusing into each other, in other ways maintaining a tense equilibrium.

As for occupational and co-subordination identities, the study's findings indicate their potential for becoming a transnational source of communication and bonding. In Isrocom, I have maintained, occupational and co-subordination ties with the merger partners included common universes of meaning that, though serving as grist for the mill of separatism, also imposed loyalty claims upon members. These were especially apparent in the ways that some members described interactions with colleagues and peers from Amerotech. Tracing out tales of such engagements, they constructed themselves in narrative as trapped between conflicting and equally commanding local and global moral demands. In other words, rather than being suppressed by the struggle for separatism, occupational and co-subordination attachments were framed as bearing deep significance for members, pressing them to justify their actions in accordance with notions of right and wrong that they shared with American colleagues and peers. In this sense, the narratives were a testament to the way that these global identities buffered the social effects of globalization, keeping them attuned to moral standards that render any other in some ways a part of any sense of self.

This study is not only concerned with the three types of identities, but also with the relationship between them. In this regard, its findings have theoretical implications not only for organizational theory, but also for a more general theory of identity. Most critically, the findings suggest that identities not only constitute objects of social construction—the main theoretical focus of Early and Symbolic Interactionists and their followers—but are also one of its central tools. As was perhaps most strongly illustrated in the analysis of the way national identity was recruited to symbolically bolster the local-organizational boundary, it appears that one identity may serve as a symbolic tool in the construction of another, its own meanings undergoing transformations in the process. Identities, in this sense, are symbolically interconnected: as one is recruited to serve the construction of another, their content flexibly shifts and fuses, and meanings flow between them. Constituting both objects and tools of social construction, identities undergo continuous interchanges in terms of whatever it means to belong.

Moreover, the analysis of the relations between the organizational and national identities also complicates existing views of social-psychology. Social psychologists typically view self-esteem as a basic motive for conceptualizations of self (for example, Rosenberg 1981), focusing primarily on the self-esteem dimension of the self-concept (Gecas 1982: 10), and arguing that even those at the very bottom of the social order generate identities that provide them with a measure of self-worth (Snow & Anderson 1987).[2] To some degree, the findings reported here are consistent with this thesis: though there were cases of condemning attitudes toward the local-organizational "us"—of self-critical judgments formed along the contours of proclaimed Israeli faults—members usually did speak of themselves in ways that aggrandized their organizational value. Yet interestingly, this aggrandizement of value derived meaning from accepting a subordinate national status. In other words, the self-attribution of superior value inside the merged organization was related to the surrendering of national status on the outside; to accepting its general inferiority. Thus it seems, that one identity may be used to bolster the worth of another, though its own status may in some ways be sacrificed in the process.

The notion that identities coexist in a state of flow and movement is to some degree consistent with postmodernist convictions. Isrocom's globalization, it seems, did introduce some of the "creative juxtapositions," "fusions," or "interpenetrations" that postmodernists often speak about in relation to identities. And yet these identity-interplays did not appear infinite, unbound, or incoherent as many of them claim. On the contrary, as members' narrated identity-dilemmas indicate, the interplay was premised on an internal, social, and moral logic of its own: incongruence was experienced as inner conflict, conflict necessitated choice, and choice needed justification. Flows and interpenetrations, in other words, fused together into particular story lines that were premised upon coherence-invoking sets of codes and constraints. Globalization, it thus seems, perhaps fragments identities to a considerable extent, but the fragments remain attached in consequential ways that set constraints upon peoples' thoughts and actions, having some ability to center their "decentered" selves.

With regard to practical implications, I leave this task to others. In contrast with what appears to be the general trend in the field, this study was not conducted with the goals of management in mind.[3] Furthermore, it seems to me that full answers to practical questions demand further analyses of later, more advanced stages of organizational mergers and also of other merger sites. However, to those who do have such practical goals in mind and to those curious about the fate of the merger partners, another fact about Isrocom should be made known. At this point in time its merger with Amerotech can be labeled a success. The corporate marriage that was romantically celebrated on the first merger day, but that quickly turned into a struggle for separateness, did not end in a divorce. Globalint, at the time of writing, still exists. The company overcame some of the hardships that plagued the high-tech sector in general, and, moreover, registered some notable business achievements. Indeed, since the merger between Isrocom and Amerotech, Com, the parent-company, pursued several other acquisitions. The gifts of "Global Capitalism" have thus been bestowed upon this company even though globalism itself had in many ways been rejected by it.

Those who nonetheless insist on the need to monitor identities in global contexts seem to have their hands full. As this study shows, identities are far more complex than cognitive, objective essences that can be studied through pen-and-pencil comparisons or elegantly engineered to overcome friction. They are, ultimately, a social product, one that flexibly springs from and creatively reappropriates the foundations of the global regime of work. The united structures, the integrated technology, the re-established routines, even the sweet romanticism and rosy clichés—all managerial attempts to shape loyalties and manufacture attachments—cannot determine members' identities, certainly not in any clear-cut or direct manner. They themselves become objects of and means for social construction and are continually molded and remolded to fit an ongoing, often ironic and paradoxical process of negotiating boundaries of belonging and their meaning.

But what may be less manageable than is assumed by those seeking to control global organizations, may be more manageable than is imagined by those working within them. As more and more organizations undergo globalization, more and more people face the necessity of working with others of a different national origin. For them, the impediments of international communication within organizations may become a serious problem that threatens the quality of everyday work-life. This problem, the study shows, is not so much that of a big identity-gap that people have difficulty overcoming, as of small differences that people insist on preserving. So eager to side with an "us," members easily lose sight of how the boundary they come to view as natural is to a large extent a product of their own making; of their own, however unwitting or unmindful, attempts to exclude and devalue. For those engaged in global endeavors of this sort, Isrocom's case should serve as a reminder of this, as well as of another, interrelated fact: that every member of a "them" might also be—at the same time or through the slightest change in the situation—also a member of another, crosscutting "us." Multiple identities, in other words, imply multiple paths for communication and bonding. Through them those merged apart could perhaps find a global way.

Notes

Notes to Chapter 1

1. The names of the company, its merger partner, parent company, and the united company are all disguised. Various identifying details pertaining to them, as well as to the people who are studied in this book, have also been altered. The names that are used in this book—namely, "Isrocom" (Israeli Online Communication Company), "Amerotech" (American Online Technology Company), "Com," and "Globalint" (Globally Integrated Company)—have all been invented for the purpose of this book, and have no link whatsoever to any company or companies other than those they are intended to disguise.
2. "Mazel Tov" is Hebrew for "congratulations."
3. For estimates and evaluations, as well as for discussions of the problems encountered in international mergers and acquisitions, see for example, Child, Faulkner & Pitkethly (2001) and Sóderberg & Vaara (2003). See Stearns & Allan (1996) and Aley & Siegel (1998) for estimates focusing on mergers and acquisitions in the United States.
4. "Local" as it is used in this study implies that which is confined to a specific territory. While often equivalent to the term "national," "local" is not used here as its synonym. On the contrary, the relationship between the two terms is one of the issues of analysis and discussion.
5. See, for example, Ross & Trachte's (1990) *Global Capitalism: The New Leviathan* for a discussion of the economic characteristics of this new phase. It should be noted, that although the contemporary economic system does not mark a complete "de-territorialism" of all economic processes (see for example Sassen 1991; Saxenian 1994), it does mark a new productive regionalism. Driven by international capital movements and universal economic rationale (Gereffi 1994), it slices through traditional frontiers (see in this regard Henderson 1989).
6. For more thorough discussions of the spatial dispersion of high-tech companies, its causes and consequences see Flamm (1985), Castells (1989), Henderson (1989), Saxenian (1994), and Ó Riain (1997).
7. One of the most famous proponents of this essentialist view seems to be Erik Erikson. See his well-known *Identity and the Life Cycle* (1959/1980) and its influential conceptualization of identity as self-sameness.
8. The search for identity did not, of course, begin with contemporary globalization. See for example Klapp's (1969) *Collective Search for Identity* for an

analysis of how earlier, modernist signs of social disjuncture led to a quest for symbolically and emotionally potent collective identities among American youth movements in the 1960s. See also Cohen's (1982; 1986) discussions of the ways that local British communities upon which municipal, economical, or political definitions of collectivity were imposed constructed and became aware of their joint identity at its boundaries.

9. "Identity" is hereby defined as *a definition of self as belonging to a group of others, as well as the meanings attributed to this belonging in terms of the designation of the group, the self, and the relationship between them.* This definition constitutes a certain combination of various related concepts that are commonly used in literature: "self-concept" and "self schema" (see Tedeschi, Linskold, Rosenfeld 1985); "personal identity," "collective identity," and "social identity" (see Jenkins 1996). With regard to the former two, "identity" as it is used here implies a self-concept (see for example Markus & Kunda 1986) that concerns group belonging and its accompanying self schemas (Markus 1977). With regard to the latter three, "identity" as it is used here implies *personal* definitions of *collective* belongings. It captures the concept "social identity," namely other people's perceptions of us (Goffman 1959; Tedeschi et al. 1985), only to the degree that these perceptions are internalized as our own. It should also be mentioned that though the study focuses on the organizational identity—on definitions of self as belonging to an *organizational* group of others—other identities are also scrutinized. Namely, Chapter 5 deals with national identity and Chapter 6 deals with occupational and co-subordination identities.

10. Specifically, these researchers examine issues that concern its fit to members' existing self-conceptions, needs, or preferences (Dutton, Dukerich & Harquail 1994) or, conversely, its effects upon members' behavior: upon the way that they enact their roles (Golden-Biddle & Rao 1997), for example, or the way that they respond to organizational problems (Dutton & Dukerich 1991), external status threats (Elsbach & Kramer 1996), and induced change (Reger, Gustafson, Demarie & Mullane 1994; Gioia & Thomas 1996).

11. For another example, this time relating to a Japanese high-tech work team, see Kilduff, Funk & Mehra (1997).

12. For a thorough review of this and other interactionist schools of thought see Reynolds (1987).

13. Among the most well-known are "Symbolic Interactionists" Blumer (1969) and Hughes (1958) of the Chicago School. They have each contributed to the insights of the "Early Interactionists," the former by supplementing them with methodological vigor, and the latter by applying them to the study of occupational and professional, racial and ethnic identities.

14. The relationships between a person's multiple identities will be further elaborated in the chapters that follow, especially Chapters 5 and 6. With regard to Goffman, see his discussion about personal and "ego or felt" identities in *Stigma* (1963). The former is claimed to have a "one-of-a-kind" quality (footnote, p. 62) that is based on "positive marks or identity pegs, and the unique combination of life history items that comes to be attached to the individual with the help of these pegs for his identity" (p. 57), while the latter concerns the

"subjective sense of his own situation and his own continuity and character that an individual comes to obtain as a result of his various social experiences" (p. 105). See Weigert (1983) for a more thorough discussion of Goffman's as well as other "sociological social psychologists'" treatment of "identity."

15. It is interesting that of all researchers, two of the most famous proponents of the notion of social construction, Berger and Luckmann (1966), limit rather than widen the notion of identity's socially constructed nature. As Weigert (1983) points out, they see identity as a social meaning constructed like other meanings, but with the uniquely existential dimension of being anchored in an individual's body. While admitting that historically available types of identity are nothing but social, actual personal identity is, for them, a dialectically generated social reality vivified in individual experience and anchored in actual, individual bodies (see p. 193).

16. So much so, that for many postmodernists the contemporary era marks "the death of the 'self,'" the tearing off of the disguises that conceal its "naturalized, artificial origins" (Levine 1992: 1, 2). It brings to light "the story of (self's) debunking, its fragmentation, its dismemberment, its explosion, dissolution, destruction, its scattering or dispersal, and, finally, its annihilation" (Gloege 1992: 59). Nevertheless, as Sass (1992) eloquently claims, "even in these quarters—the realms of 'postmodernism' and 'post-structuralism'—selfhood remains a central obsession: . . . many who claim to disbelieve in the self seem to take an inordinate delight in dancing round its burning image" (p. 17).

17. On the need to maintain synchronous self-images see, for example, Van Maanen (1979), Markus (1977; 1983), Greenwald (1980), Swann & Hill (1982). Some postmodernists, it should be noted, do not accept this notion of a "need." See discussion in Chapter 5.

18. Both Hochschild (1983) and Kondo (1990), it should be noted, dealt with the interrelation between organizational membership and gender identities.

19. The cross-cultural field is to a large extent a part or an extension of a body of research that deals with diversity in organizations. While the former focuses primarily on national difference in international organizational settings, the latter focuses on the ways that various categories of difference (such as race, gender, ethnicity, sexual orientation, social class, age, and so forth) come into play in organizations (that are usually not international). Furthermore, while the former highlights the implications of between-group differences in culture, the latter also applies a categorization or labeling approach to the study of difference in organizations (Ferdman 1995). It is noteworthy that diversity researchers, like cross-cultural researchers, seem to recognize the interconnectedness between a person's multiple identities in that their concern is often with the effects of diversity upon members' sense of attachment to the organization (for example, Tsui, Egan & O'Reilly III 1992). By the same token, their handling of this interconnectedness seems to be characterized by the same drawbacks that will soon be specified with regard to cross-cultural research.

20. Based both on inter- and intraorganizational comparisons, findings show, for example, that national identities are perpetuated in ways workers resist change (Harzing & Hofstede 1996) and in their reactions to various kinds

of leadership behavior (Kanungo & Mendonca 1996); that cultural diversity is sustained even within the same small work group, consequently effecting its processes and outcomes (Thomas, Ravlin & Wallace 1996); and that there is variance in the effectiveness of various managerial and motivational techniques in different countries (Erez & Earley 1993). Moreover, the work of various cross-cultural writers indicates that national identities remain influential not only with regard to workers, but with regard to managers as well (see Peterson 1993; Hickson & Pugh 1995). Even though they face the same global environment and seek the same goal of profit, differences between national cultures are perpetuated, for example, in managers' preferences for allocating scarce resources (Dukerich, Golden & Jacobson 1996); in their perception of and response to constraints such as uncertainty (Peterson, Elliott, Bliese & Radford 1996); in their propensity to form technological alliances (Steensma, Marino, Weaver & Dickson 2000); in the type of change strategy they prefer (Harzing & Hofstede 1996); in the way they organize certain stages of product development (Ettlie, Dreher, Kovacs & Trygg 1994); and in the individual interactions they are likely to form when establishing international joint ventures (Olk & Earley 1996). In sum, cross-cultural researchers find that national identities are perpetuated and manifested in the behavior of both workers and managers of the global organization.

21. See Tayeb (1994; 2001) and Roberts & Boyacigiller (1984) for other methodological and perceptual problems that characterize cross-cultural studies.

22. It is often claimed that while female ethnographers become "honorary males" when studying alien cultures, their gender somehow inconspicuous in relation to much more striking differences, when conducting research "at home" gender becomes a critical "specification marker" (Hastrup 1987). The behavior of a female fieldworker is consequently more closely scrutinized than that of a male (see Mascarenhas-Keyes 1987). While I was, in a broad sense, culturally at home, an Israeli studying other Israelis, in the first half of fieldwork I did not feel this problematic in my case. I was visibly pregnant at that time, and, surprisingly perhaps, pregnancy proved to be an excellent icebreaker, inspiring not only friendliness and talk, but also cooperation on the part of both women and men. Despite the fact that this was an "anthropology at home" (Jackson 1987), I felt that, if anything, my gender eased my way around the organization, at least during the first six months of fieldwork.

23. Translation seems to hold the potential for worsening some of the existing problems of ethnographic presentation (for a discussion of such problems see Van Maanen 1995). I was very careful in this regard. Furthermore, it should be noted that this potential shortcoming has to a large extent been balanced by an important advantage: since this study focuses on identity as a social construct, my ability to distance myself from the vehicle of construction, language (Sarup 1996: 48), seemed to have greatly helped in gaining insight into what was said.

24. The following writers refer to transnational corporations as one of the sites from which globalization evolves and develops: Appadurai (1990), Sklair (1991), and Hannerz (1996).

Notes to Chapter Two

1. This was cited in a Hebrew newspaper article.
2. Blue and white are the colors of the Israeli flag. They symbolize things Israeli.
3. Globalint had a complex matrix structure that consisted of both geographical departments acting as independent profit units and functional departments responsible for certain functions or areas of expertise.
4. Since Isrocom's structure constituted a complex and sometimes ambiguous matrix, the following specifications are something of a simplification. They describe the underlying logic of the structure and the major ways it was transformed as a consequence of the merger.
5. Another marketing department—"Corporate Marketing"—was centered in Amerotech and thus is not included in the scope of this study.
6. In the cases of joint sales teams, there was usually a division of labor: if Net (Isrocom's product) was presented to a client then project managers from Isrocom would present the product and those from Amerotech would present background information about the company. If Amerotech's product was marketed, then the division of labor would be the other way around.
7. The distinction between these two kinds of R&D workers was often blurred. For example, there was high turnover among many of the full members just as there were cases of freelancers who stayed with the company for years, became an integral part of work teams, and participated in all of the organizationally sponsored events.
8. Group mergers took diverse forms. Isrocom's Americas and Asia Pacific support groups were subordinated, without other substantial structural changes, to the manager of the parallel groups in New York. Furthermore, both of the integrated groups were further subordinated, through a matrix structure, to the managers of the regional marketing departments. The EMEA group remained basically local and mostly unchanged. With regard to the functional groups, an Amerotech group was added to the local department's existing structure, and the rest of the functional groups were integrated and subordinated either to local managers or, on rare occasions, to joint matrix managers from both sites.
9. Two additions to this global technological infrastructure were added after the first year of merger, and thus after the field study was completed: a video conferencing utility and a joint ERP (Enterprise Resource Planning) system.
10. Survey questions included statements about the way the companies handle employees (for example, "The company is loyal to its employees and looks out for their best interest at all times"); statements about the way it handles

its business (for example, "My company does a good job at long term planning"), and a few statements about the behavior of coworkers (for example, "Employees in my work group are willing to work long hours to achieve tasks and goals required in order to meet established delivery dates/goals").

Notes to Chapter Three

1. To a large extent, Barth (1969) is one of the first to focus on intergroup difference rather than intragroup similarity in conceptualizations of identity. For a discussion of this approach, see Chapter 1.
2. In contrast to English, Hebrew is written from right to left.
3. See De Vries' (1997) historical analysis of Jewish clerks in British-ruled Palestine for another example of how the Israeli identity was used as a symbolic resource in an identity-construction process.
4. This finding concurs with the insights of the Early and Symbolic Interactionists (see Chapter 1), which generally seem to have been neglected or overlooked by contemporary postmodernism.

Notes to Chapter Four

1. The Israeli law requires that homes and buildings have war-shelters built within them for times of emergency.
2. It should be mentioned that most of the department's employees, and, for that matter, most of Isrocom's employees were secular Jews. The relation between the Jewish identity and the Israeli identity will be further discussed in the next chapter.
3. In their study of the significance of photographs in corporate annual reports of American computer firms, Dougherty & Kunda (1990) also speak of the self-conscious tales these photos tell about firms. Taking it a step forward, Guthey & Jackson (2005) speak of the ambiguous relationship between photographs of CEOs and the process of identity construction. Namely, they argue that these powerful means for self-consciously constructing corporate identity and image give rise to an "authenticity paradox": while trying to convey an impression of authentic presence, they actually lay bare the elusiveness of authenticity in this realm, if not its impossibility.

Notes to Chapter Five

1. In the realm of academic discourse, the notion of "integrated self" was made famous by Erik Erikson (1959/1980). This notion was seriously challenged by various writers working well within modernist bounds. Examples of critiques

of the notion of a coherent, solid self include Gergen (1972), Van Maanen (1979), Markus & Kunda (1986).

2. In correspondence to the above argument, researchers of Israeli society claim that the Israeli sense of "oneness" is construed, to a large extent, in relations to different collective others (Dominguez 1989). Alongside the image of the historic Diaspora Jew, researchers have often focused upon the key constituting role of the image of the Arab-other which, in the context of the perpetual Israeli-Palestinian conflict, became a dominant pole against which a wide variety of identity constructs have been developed, ranging from that of the "enlightened," modern, democratic Jewish-Israeli (for example, Dominguez 1989; Eyal 1996; Khazzoom 2003) to religious brands of militant nationalism (see Kimmerling 2001).

3. For a review of various views about the Americanization of Israel see Abramson's (2000) introduction to a special issue focusing on this topic in *Israel Studies* (volume 5, number 1).

4. The negative conception was expressed in approximately fifteen percent of the interviews.

5. See Ben-Ari & Bilu (1997) for various analyses of other meanings attributed to space and place in contemporary Israeli discourses.

6. Some citizen groups, such as Arabs and Orthodox Jews, are relieved from mandatory army service.

7. "Tzabar" is slang for native-born Israeli.

8. The existence of a mental schema of global hierarchy has also been reported in Ben-Ari's (1996) study of Japanese business expatriates in Singapore.

9. See Chapter 2.

10. Thus, most evidently, the founding fathers and inventors of Zionism chose the religiously preserved collective memory of the ancient Holy Land as the territorial base of their nation and state building effort, revitalized the Biblical Hebrew, and adopted the Bible as the primary mythical infrastructure for a new historiography of Judaism as nationality (Kimmerling 2001: especially pp. 4; 186). To this day, Jewish religious elements have been incorporated into several laws such as those restricting employment and public transportation on the Shabbath and regulations of Kashrut. Additionally, for Jews, personal status issues are under the jurisdiction of rabbinical courts. It should nevertheless be noted, that there are also Islamic Shari'a courts and courts operating according to Christian denomination rules. Legally, Israel is not a single state religion, and Judaism is but one of fourteen established and state-supported religions (Dowty 1998: 161).

11. There are, furthermore, deep historic tensions between the secular and the religious concerning the issue of relations between religion and state. See for example Dowty (1998: chapter 8) and Sharkansky (1996: chapter 5).

12. In his study of a European subsidiary of LEGO, Karmark (2002) also documented members' attempts to resist the formal ideology by claiming the subsidiary a better version of it ("More Lego than Lego"). Although his research focuses on different questions than those studied here, this finding nevertheless

resonates with what is presented. To a large extent, it lends further support to the claim that it is not some kind of "essential Israeliness" that expressed itself through the fact of members' resistance, but an Israeliness symbolically constructed for an internal, social, and political struggle that apparently exists—in one form or other—in other organizations as well.

Notes to Chapter Six

1. Identifying themselves with their occupation (Becker & Carper 1956; Hughes 1958), occupational members are claimed to be committed to the values, norms, and perspectives that establish their knowledge as "expertise" (see Abbott 1991) and extend beyond work-related matters (Van Maanen & Barley 1984). Furthermore, often acting in solidarity with their occupational colleagues, members take part in an effort to justify their work to themselves and to others (Fine 1996; Wacquant 1995; De Vries 1997), as well as to further their status, power, and autonomy in the occupational and organizational division of labor (for example, Abbott 1988; Freidson 1986; Weitz & Shenhav 2000; Shenhav & Weitz 2000). See Barley & Kunda (2004) for a recent account of how occupational communities transcend traditional organizations, binding together "itinerant experts"—technical professionals working as contractors—in the high-tech knowledge economy. See Hannerz (1996) and Ben-Ari & Elron (2001) for accounts of how occupational ties transcend spatial bounds, binding together professionals from all over the world.

2. It should be clarified that in my discussion about co-subordination I am *not* referring to class identities. Co-subordination identity could, in my account, be characteristic of anyone who is employed in the organization, including managers or executives, as long as they are subordinated to a common source of authority.

3. It is true, that as sophisticated schemes of managerial control threaten to take ahold of members' deep, underlying sense of self (Kunda 1992; Hochschild 1983) and as they govern more and more aspects of the ways members lead their lives (Whyte 1956; Mills 1956), the experience of subordination—of the boundary that sets apart those who are subordinated from those who are their subordinators—is at least to some degree challenged, obscured, or made ambivalent. Nonetheless, regardless of developments in forms of control, the workplace has apparently remained a "contested terrain" (Edwards 1979). As Kunda (1992) claims, even in the most advanced form of normative control members maintain some ability to detach themselves from and adopt a critical stance toward the organization, albeit in a partial and ambiguous way. Such detachment also has its more collective manifestations. Studies of various work contexts indicate, for example, that workers discursively reappropriate organizational ideology in ways that register protest (Kondo 1990), and that they develop subgroups with norms that often run counter to organizational expectations (see for example Burawoy 1979; Homans 1950; Roethlisberger & Dickson 1939; Roy 1959). Moreover, such resistance and disengagement is documented with

respect to organizational subordinates of all kinds, even those who are also, to a large extent, the agents of control, namely managers and executives (for example, Whyte 1956; Dalton 1959; Jackall 1988; Mills 1956).

4. For elaboration see Chapter 2 (Setting).

5. These titles constitute somewhat loosely defined occupations that were derived from emic, first order definitions. Project managers were technical professionals who had made a career move into marketing, usually after the completion of an MBA or in the course of studying it. Computer programmers were software developers, usually with a BA degree in computer science. Human resource workers and managers had less of a common academic background, and their occupation was defined more in terms of their organizational title and line of work.

6. This view was reviewed in detail in the Introduction (Chapter 1).

Notes to Chapter Seven

1. In this regard, see, for example, Gioia & Thomas (1996); Scott & Lane (2000); Gioia, Schultz & Corley (2000); Brown & Starkey (2000).

2. This conviction, by the way, had been integrated into mainstream theoretical notions of the organizational identity as well. See, for example, Dutton et al. (1994).

3. See for example Barley, Meyer & Gash's (1988) systematic documentation of the way the practitioner subculture has influenced academic discourse on organizational culture.

References

Abbott, Andrew. 1988. *The System of Professions: An Essay on the Division of Expert Labor.* Chicago: The University of Chicago Press.

Abbott, Andrew. 1991. "The Future of Professions: Occupation and Expertise in the Age of Organization." *Research in the Sociology of Organizations* 8: 17–42.

Abramson, Glenda. 2000. "Introduction." *Israel Studies* 5, no. 1: vii-xii.

Agar, Michael H. 1996. *The Professional Stranger.* 2nd edition. San Diego, CA: Academic Press.

Ailon, Galit. Forthcoming. "Mirror, Mirror on the Wall: *Culture's Consequences* in a Value Test of its Own Design." Academy of Management Review.

Ailon-Souday, Galit and Gideon Kunda. 2003. "The Local Selves of Global Workers: The Social Construction of National Identity in the Face of Organizational Globalization." *Organization Studies* 24, no. 7: 1073–1096.

Albert, Stuart, and David A. Whetten. 1985. "Organizational Identity." In *Research in Organizational Behavior* 7: 263–295.

Aley, James, and Matt Siegel. 1998. "Why the Deals Keep Coming: The Fallout from Merger Mania." *Fortune,* March 16: 14–15.

Anderson, Benedict. 1983. *Imagined Communities: Reflections on the Origin and Spread of Nationalism.* London: Verso.

Appadurai, Arjun. 1990. "Disjuncture and Difference in the Global Cultural Economy." *Theory, Culture & Society* 7: 295–310.

Arieli, Daniella. 2001. *Outsiders in China: The World of Western Expatriates Living in Beijing in the End of the 90s.* Unpublished Dissertation, The Hebrew University in Jerusalem (in Hebrew).

Azaryahu, Maoz. 2000. "McIsrael? On the 'Americanization of Israel.'" *Israel Studies* 5, no. 1: 41–64.

Bacharach, Samuel B., Peter A. Bamberger, and Miriam Erez. 1996. "The Cross-Cultural Analysis of Organizations: Bridging the Micro-Macro and Ideographic-Nomothetic Gaps." *Research in the Sociology of Organizations* 14: vii-xiv.

Barley, Stephen R. and Gideon Kunda. 2004. *Gurus, Hired guns, and Warm Bodies: Itinerant Experts in a Knowledge Economy.* Princeton: Princeton University Press.

Barley, Stephen R., Gordon W. Meyer, and Debra C. Gash. 1988. "Cultures of Culture: Academics, Practitioners and the Pragmatics of Normative Control." *Administrative Science Quarterly* 33: 24–60.

Barth, Fredrik. 1969. *Ethnic Groups and Boundaries.* Boston: Little, Brown and Company.

Bauman, Zygmunt. 1998. *Globalization: The Human Consequences.* NY: Columbia University Press.

Becker, Howard S., and James Carper. 1956. "The Elements of Identification with an Occupation." *American Sociological Review* 21, no. 3: 341–348.

Beit-Hallahmi, Benjamin, and Zvi Sobel. 1991. "Introduction." In *Jewishness and Judaism in Contemporary Israel,* eds. Zvi Sobel and Benjamin Beit-Hallahmi. Albany: State University of New York Press, pp. 1–22.

Ben-Ari, Eyal, and Efrat Elron. 2001. "Blue Helmets and White Armor: Multi-Nationalism and Multi-Culturalism Among UN Peacekeeping Forces." *City & Society* XIII, no. 2: 271–302.

Ben-Ari, Eyal, and Yoram Bilu (eds.). 1997. *Grasping Land.* Albany: State University of New York Press.

Ben-Ari, Eyal. 1996. "Globalization, 'Folk Models' of the World Order and National Identity: Japanese Business Expatriates in Singapore." *Social Sciences Research Centre Occasional Paper* 18. Hong Kong: The Social Sciences Research Centre, the University of Hong Kong, in association with the Department of Sociology, The University of Hong Kong.

Ben-Rafael, Eliezer. 2005. "From Religion to Nationalism: The Transformation of the Jewish Identity." In *Comparing Modernities: Pluralism versus Homogeneity,* eds. Eliezer Ben-Rafael and Yitzhak Sternberg. Leiden: Brill, pp. 365–392.

Berger, Peter L., and Thomas Luckmann. 1966. *The Social Construction of Reality.* Garden City, NY: Doubleday.

Bhabha, Homi K. 1990. "Introduction: Narrating the Nation." In Homi K. Bhabha, *Nation and Narration.* London: Routledge.

Bhabha, Homi K. 1994. *The Location of Culture.* London: Routledge.

Biggart, Nicole Woolsey. 1977. "The Creative-Destructive Process of Organizational Change: The Case of the Post Office." *Administrative Science Quarterly* 22 (September): 410–426.

Blumer, Herbert. 1969. *Symbolic Interactionism: Perspective and the Method.* Englewood Cliffs, NJ: Prentice-Hall.

Brown, Andrew D., and Ken Starkey. 2000. "Toward Integration." *The Academy of Management Review* 25: 148–150.

Burawoy, Michael. 1979. *Manufacturing Consent: Changes in the Labor Process under Monopoly Capitalism.* Chicago: University of Chicago Press.

Burawoy, Michael. 2000. "Grounding Globalization." In *Global Ethnography: Forces, Connections, and Imaginations in a Postmodern World,* eds. Michael Burawoy et al. Berkeley: University of California Press, pp. 337–350.

Calorie, Roland; Michael Lubatkin; and Philippe Very. 1994. "Control Mechanisms in Cross-Border Acquisitions: An International Comparison." *Organization Studies* 15, no. 3: 361–380.

Castells, Manuel. 1989. *The Informational City: Information, Technology, Economic Restructuring, and the Urban-Regional Process.* Oxford: Basil Blackwell.

Child, John, David Faulkner, and Robert Pitkethly. 2001. *The Management of International Acquisitions.* Oxford: Oxford University Press.

Clark, Burton R. 1972. "The Organizational Saga in Higher Education." *Administrative Science Quarterly* 7 (June): 178–184.

Cohen, Anthony P. 1982. "Belonging: The Experience of Culture." In *Belonging: Identity and Social Organization in British Rural Cultures,* ed. Anthony P. Cohen. Manchester: Manchester University Press, pp. 1–17.

Cohen, Anthony P. 1985. *The Symbolic Construction of Community.* London: Tavistock.

Cohen, Anthony P. 1986. "Of Symbols and Boundaries, or, Does Ertie's Greatcoat Hold the Key?" In *Symbolising Boundaries: Identity and Diversity in British Cultures,* ed. Anthony P. Cohen. Manchester: Manchester University Press, pp. 1–19.

Cooley, Charles Horton. 1902. *Human Nature and the Social Order.* NY: Charles Scribner's Sons.

Czarniawska, Barbara. 1997. *Narrating the Organization: Dramas of Institutional Identity.* Chicago: The University of Chicago Press.

Dalton, Melville. 1959. *Men Who Manage: Fusions of Feeling and Theory in Administration.* New York: J. Wiley.

De Vries, David. 1997. "National Construction of Occupational Identity: Jewish Clerks in British-Ruled Palestine." *Comparative Studies in Society and History* 39, number 2 (April): 373–400.

Denzin, Norman K. 1994. "The Art and Politics of Interpretation." In *Handbook of Qualitative Research,* eds. Normal K. Denzin and Yvonna S. Lincoln. Thousand Oaks: Sage, pp. 500–515.

Derrida, Jacques. 1981. *Positions.* Chicago: University of Chicago Press.

Dominguez, Virginia R. 1989. *People as Subject, People as Object: Selfhood and Peoplehood in Contemporary Israel.* Madison: University of Wisconsin Press.

Dougherty, Debra, and Gideon Kunda. 1990. "Photograph Analysis: A Method to Capture Organizational Belief Systems." In *Symbols and Artefacts: Views of the Corporate Landscape,* ed. P. Pasquale. Berlin: Walter de Gruyter, pp. 185–206.

Dowty, Alan. 1998. *The Jewish State: A Century Later.* Berkeley: University of California Press.

Dukerich, Janet M., Brian R. Golden, and Carol K. Jacobson. 1996. "Nested Cultures and Identities: A Comparative Study of Nation and Profession/Occupation Status Effects on Resource Allocation Decisions." *Research in the Sociology of Organizations* 14: 35–89.

Dutton, Jane E., and Janet M. Dukerich. 1991. "Keeping an Eye on the Mirror: Image and Identity in Organizational Adaptation." *Academy of Management Journal* 34, no. 3: 517–554.

Dutton, Jane E., Janet M. Dukerich, and Celia V. Harquail. 1994. "Organizational Images and Member Identification." *Administrative Science Quarterly* 39: 239–263.

Edwards, Richard. 1979. *Contested Terrain: The Transformation of the Workplace in the Twentieth Century.* New York: Basic Books.

Elsbach, Kimberly D., and Roderick M. Kramer. 1996. "Members' Responses to Organizational Identity Threats: Encountering and Countering the *Business Week* Rankings." *Administrative Science Quarterly* 41: 442–476.

Erez, Miriam, and P. Christopher Earley. 1993. *Culture, Self Identity and Work.* NY: Oxford University Press.

Erikson, Erik H. 1980 (1959). *Identity and the Life Cycle.* A re-issue. New York: Norton and Company.

Ettlie, John E., Carsten Dreher, George L. Kovacs, and Lars Trygg. 1994. "Cross-National Comparisons of Product Development in Manufacturing." *Advances in Global High-Technology Management* 4 Part B: 91–109.

Eyal, Gil. 1996. "The Discursive Origins of Israeli Separatism: The Case of the Arab Village." *Theory and Society* 25, no. 3: 389–429.

Featherstone, Mike. 1990. "Global Culture: An Introduction." *Theory, Culture & Society* 7: 1–14.

Featherstone, Mike. 1995. *Undoing Culture: Globalization, Postmodernism and Identity.* London: Sage Publications.

Ferdman, Bernardo M. 1995. "Cultural Identity and Diversity in Organizations: Bridging the Gap Between Group Differences and Individual Uniqueness." In *Diversity in Organizations: New Perspectives for a Changing Workplace*, eds. Martin M. Chemers, Stuart Oskamp, and Mark A. Costanzo. Thousand Oaks: Sage, pp. 37–61.

Fine, Gary Alan. 1996. "Justifying Work: Occupational Rhetorics as Resources in Restaurant Kitchens." *Administrative Science Quarterly* 41: 90–115.

Flamm, Kenneth. 1985. "Internationalization in the Semiconductor Industry." In Joseph Grunwald and Kenneth Flamm (eds.), *The Global Factory: Foreign Assembly in International Trade*. Washington, D.C.: The Brookings Institution, pp. 38–136.

Foucault, Michel. 1980. *Power/Knowledge: Selected Interviews and Other Writings, 1972–1977*, ed. Colin Gordon. Brighton: Harvestor.

Freidson, Eliot. 1986. *Professional Powers: A Study on the Institutionalization of Formal Knowledge.* Chicago: The University of Chicago Press.

Frenkel, Michal, and Yehouda Shenhav. 2003. "From Americanization to Colonization: The Diffusion of Productivity Models Revisited." *Organization Studies* 24, no. 9: 1523–1561.

Gecas, Viktor. 1982. "The Self Concept." *Annual Review of Sociology* 8: 1–33.

Geertz, Clifford. 1973. *The Interpretation of Cultures.* USA: Basic Books.

Gereffi, Gary. 1994. "The International Economy and Economic Development." In *The Handbook of Economic Sociology*, eds. Neil J. Smelser and Richard Swedberg. Princeton: Princeton University Press/Russel Sage Foundation, pp. 206–233.

Gergen, Kenneth J. 1972. "Multiple Identity: The Healthy, Happy Human Being Wears Many Masks." *Psychology Today* 5, no. 12 (May): 31–35; 64–66.

Gergen, Kenneth J. 1991. *The Saturated Self: Dilemmas of Identity in Contemporary Life.* USA: Basic Books.

Gioia, Dennis A., and James B. Thomas. 1996. "Identity, Image, and Issue Interpretation: Sensemaking during Strategic Change in Academia." *Administrative Science Quarterly* 41: 370–403.

Gioia, Dennis A., Majken Schultz, and Kevin G. Corley. 2000. "Organizational Identity, Image, and Adaptive Instability." *The Academy of Management Review* 25: 63–81.

Gloege, Martin E. 1992. "The American Origins of the Postmodern Self." In G. Levine (ed.), *Constructions of Self*. New Brunswick, NJ: Rutgers University Press, pp. 57–79.

Goffman, Erving. 1959. *The Presentation of Self in Everyday Life*. Garden City, NY: Doubleday.

Goffman, Erving. 1961. *Asylums: Essays on the Social Situation of Mental Patients and Other Inmates*. Garden City, New York: Anchor Books.

Goffman, Erving. 1963. *Stigma: Notes on the Management of Spoiled Identity*. Englewood Cliffs, NJ: Prentice Hall.

Golden-Biddle, Karen, and Hayagreeva Rao. 1997. "Breaches in the Boardroom: Organizational Identity and Conflicts of Commitment in a Nonprofit Organization." *Organization Science* 8, no. 6: 593–611.

Graham, Laurie. 1995. *On the Line at Subaru-Isuzu*. Ithaca: ILR Press.

Greenwald, Anthony G. 1980. "The Totalitarian Ego: Fabrication and Revision of Personal History." *American Psychologist* 35, no. 7 (July): 603–618.

Gupta, Akhil, and James Ferguson. 1992. "Beyond 'Culture': Space, Identity, and the Politics of Difference." *Cultural Anthropology* 7, no. 1: 6–23.

Guthey, Eric, and Brad Jackson. 2005. "CEO Portraits and the Authenticity Paradox." *Journal of Management Studies* 42, no. 5 (July): 1057–1082.

Hall, S. 1990. "Cultural Identity and Diaspora." In J. Rutherford (ed.) *Identity: Community, Culture, Difference*. London: Lawrence and Wishart, 222–237.

Hall, Stuart. 1996. "The Question of Cultural Identity." In *Modernity: An Introduction to Modern Societies*, eds. Stuart Hall, David Held, Don Hubert, and Kenneth Thompson. Malden, Massachusetts: Blackwell, pp. 595–634.

Hall, Stuart. 1996b. "Ethnicity: Identity and Difference." In *Becoming National*, eds. Geoff Eley and Ronald Grigor Suny. Oxford: Oxford University Press, pp. 339–349.

Hall, Stuart. 1997. "The Spectacle of the 'Other.'" In *Representation: Cultural Representation and Signifying Practices*, ed. Stuart Hall. London: Sage, pp. 223–290.

Hall, Stuart. 1997b. "The Work of Representation." In *Representation: Cultural Representation and Signifying Practices*, ed. Stuart Hall. London: Sage, pp. 13–74.

Hamada, Tomoko. 1991. *American Enterprise in Japan*. Albany: State University of New York Press.

Hamilton, Peter. 1997. "Representing the Social: France and Frenchness in Post-War Humanist Photography." In *Representation: Cultural Representation and Signifying Practices*, ed. Stuart Hall. London: Sage, 75–150.

Hannerz, Ulf. 1996. *Transnational Connections*. London: Routledge.

Harzing, Anne-Wil, and Geert Hofstede. 1996. "Planned Change in Organizations: The Influence of National Culture." *Research in the Sociology of Organizations* 14: 297–340.

Hastrup, Kirsten. 1987. "Fieldwork Among Friends: Ethnographic Exchange within the Northern Civilization." In *Anthropology at Home*, ed. Anthony Jackson. London: Tavistock Publications, pp. 94–106.

Henderson, Jeffrey William. 1989. *The Globalization of High Technology Production*. London: Routledge.

Hickson, David J., and Derek S. Pugh. 1995. *Management Worldwide: The Impact of Societal Culture on Organizations Around the Globe*. London: Penguin Books.

Hochschild, Arlie R. 1983. *The Managed Heart: Commercialization of Human Feeling*. Berkeley: University of California Press.

Hofstede, Geert. 1980. *Culture's Consequences: International Differences in Work-Related Values*. Beverly Hills: Sage Publications.

Hofstede, Geert. 1991. *Cultures and Organizations: Software of the Mind*. London: McGraw-Hill.

Hofstede, Geert. 2001. *Culture's Consequences: Comparing Values, Behaviors, Institutions, and Organizations across Nations*. 2nd Edition. Thousand Oaks, CA: Sage.

Homans, George Casper. 1950. *The Human Group*. New York: Harcourt, Brace and World.

Hughes, Everett Cherrington. 1958. *Men and Their Work*. USA: The Free Press of Glencoe.

Jack, Gavin, and Anna Lorbiecki. 2003. "Asserting Possibilities of Resistance in the Cross-Cultural Teaching Machine: Re-Viewing Videos of Others." In *Postcolonial Theory and Organizational Analysis: A Critical Engagement*, ed. Anshuman Prasad. NY: Palgrave Macmillan, pp. 213–231.

Jackall, Robert. 1988. *Moral Mazes: The World of Corporate Managers*. New York: Oxford University Press.

Jackson, Anthony (ed.) 1987. *Anthropology at Home*. London: Tavistock Publications.

Jenkins, Richard. 1996. *Social Identity*. London: Routledge.

Jermier, John M., David Knights, and Walter R. Nord. 1994. "Introduction: Resistance and Power in Organizations: Agency, Subjectivity and the Labor Process." In *Resistance and Power in Organizations*, eds. John M. Jermier, David Knights, and Walter R. Nord. London: Routledge, pp. 1–24.

Kanungo, Rabindra N., and Manuel Mendonca. 1996. "Cultural Contingencies and Leadership in Developing Countries." *Research in the Sociology of Organizations* 14: 263–298.

Karmark, Esben. 2002. *Organizational Identity in a Dualistic Subculture: A Case Study of Organizational Identity Formation in LEGO Media International*. Unpublished Dissertation, Copenhagen Business School.

Katriel, Tamar. 1986. *Talking Straight: Dugri Speech in Israeli Sabra*. Cambridge: Cambridge University Press.

Khazzoom, Aziza. 2003. "The Great Chain of Orientalism: Jewish Identity, Stigma Management, and Ethnic Exclusion in Israel." *American Sociological Review,* 68 (August): 481–510.

Kilduff, Martin, Jeffrey L. Funk, and Ajay Mehra. 1997. "Engineering Identity in a Japanese Factory." *Organization Science* 8, no. 6: 579–592.

Kimmerling, Baruch. 2001. *The Invention and Decline of Israeliness: State, Society, and the Military.* Berkeley: University of California Press.

King, Anthony D. (ed.) 1997. *Culture, Globalization and the World-System: Contemporary Conditions for the Representation of Identity.* Minneapolis, Minn.: University of Minnesota Press.

Klapp, Orrin Edgar. 1969. *Collective Search for Identity.* NY: Holt, Rinehart and Winston.

Kondo, Dorrine K. 1990. *Crafting Selves: Power, Gender, and Discourses of Identity in a Japanese Workplace.* Chicago: University of Chicago Press.

Kunda, Gideon. 1992. *Engineering Culture: Control and Commitment in a High-Tech Corporation.* Philadelphia: Temple University Press.

Laclau, Ernesto. 1995. "Universalism, Particularism, and the Question of Identity." In *The Identity in Question,* ed. John Rajchman. NY: Routledge, pp. 93–110.

Lavie, Smadar, and Ted Swedenburg (eds.). 1996. *Displacement, Diaspora and Geographies of Identity.* Durham: Duke University Press.

Levine, George. 1992. "Introduction: Constructivism and the Reemergent Self." In *Constructions of the Self,* ed. George Levine. New Brunswick, NJ: Rutgers University Press, pp. 1–13.

Liebman, Charles S., and Steven M. Cohen. 1990. *Two Worlds of Judaism: The Israeli and American Experiences.* New Haven: Yale University Press.

Lomsky-Feder, Edna, and Eyal Ben-Ari. 1999. *The Military and Militarism in Israeli Society.* Albany: State University of New York.

Markus, Hazel, and Ziva Kunda. 1986. "Stability and Malleability of the Self-Concept." *Journal of Personality and Social Psychology* 51, no. 4: 858–866.

Markus, Hazel. 1977. "Self-Schemata and Processing Information About the Self." *Journal of Personality and Social Psychology* 35, no. 2: 63–78.

Markus, Hazel. 1983. "Self-Knowledge: An Expanded View." *Journal of Personality* 51, no. 3: 543–565.

Mascarenhas-Keyes, Stella. 1987. "The Native Anthropologist: Constraints and Strategies in Research." In *Anthropology at Home,* ed. Anthony Jackson. London: Tavistock Publications, pp. 180–195.

Mathews, Gordon. 2000. *Global Culture/Individual Identity: Searching for Home in the Cultural Supermarket.* London: Routledge.

Mead, George Herbert. 1934. *Mind, Self, and Society.* Chicago: University of Chicago Press.

Mills, C. Wright. 1956. *White Collar.* New York: Oxford University Press.

Ó Riain, S. 1997. "An Offshore Silicon Valley? The Emerging Irish Software Industry." *Competition & Change* 2: 175–212.

Ó Riain, Seán. 2000. "Net-Working for a Living: Irish Software Developers in the Global Workplace." In *Global Ethnography: Forces, Connections, and Imaginations in a Postmodern World*, eds. Michael Burawoy et al. Berkeley: University of California Press, pp. 175–202.

Ohmae, Kenichi. 1999. *The Borderless World: Power and Strategy in the Interlinked Economy (Revised Edition)*. New York: HarperBusiness.

Ohmae, Kenichi. 1995. *The End of the Nation State: The Rise of Regional Economics*. New York: Free Press.

Olie, René. 1994. "Shades of Culture and Institutions in International Mergers." *Organization Studies* 15 (3): 381–405.

Olk, Paul, and P. Christopher Earley. 1996. "Rediscovering the Individual in the Formation of International Joint Ventures." *Research in the Sociology of Organizations* 14: 223–261.

Peterson, Mark F., James R. Elliott, Paul D. Bliese, and Mark H. B. Radford. 1996. "Profile Analysis of the Sources of Meaning Reported by U.S. and Japanese Local Managers." *Research in the Sociology of Organizations* 14: 91–148.

Peterson, Richard B. 1993. "Management: An International Perspective." In *Managers and National Culture: A Global Perspective*, ed. Richard B. Peterson. Westport, Connecticut: Quorum Books, pp. 1–13.

Pratt, Michael G., and Anat Rafaeli. 1997. "Organizational Dress as a Symbol of Multilayered Social Identities." *Academy of Management Journal* 40, no. 1: 862–898.

Ram, Uri. 2004. "Glocommodification: How the Global Consumes the Local — McDonald's in Israel." *Current Sociology* 52, no. 1: 11–31.

Raz-Krakotzkin, Amnon. 1994. "Exile within Sovereignty." *Theory and Critique* 4: 23–53 and 5: 113–132 (in Hebrew).

Reger, Rhonda K., Loren T. Gustafson, Samuel M. Demarie, and John V. Mullane. 1994. "Reframing the Organization: Why Implementing Total Quality is Easier Said than Done." *Academy of Management Review* 19, no. 3: 565–584.

Regev, Motti. 2000. "To Have a Culture of Our Own: On Israeliness and Its Variants." *Ethnic and Racial Studies* 23, no. 2: 223–247.

Reynolds, Larry T. 1987. *Interactionism: Exposition and Critique*. Dix Hills, NY: General Hall.

Richardson, Laurel. 1994. "Writing: A Method of Inquiry." In *Handbook of Qualitative Research*, eds. Normal K. Denzin and Yvonna S. Lincoln. Thousand Oaks: Sage, pp. 516–529.

Roberts, Karlene H., and Nakiye A. Boyacigiller. 1984. "Cross-National Organizational Research: The Grasp of the Blind Men." *Research in Organizational Behavior* 6: 423–475.

Robertson, Roland. 1992. *Globalization: Social Theory and Global Culture*. London: Sage Publications.

Roethlisberger, Fritz Jules, and William John Dickson. 1939. *Management and the Worker*. Cambridge, Mass.: Harvard University Press.

Rosenberg, Morris. 1981. "The Self-Concept: Social Product and Social Force." In *Social Psychology: Sociological Perspectives,* eds. Morris Rosenberg and Ralph H. Turner. New York: Basic Books, pp. 593–624.

Ross, Robert J.S., and Kent C. Trachte. 1990. *Global Capitalism: The New Leviathan.* Albany: State University of New York Press.

Roy, Donald. 1959. "Banana Time: Job Satisfaction and Informal Interaction." *Human Organization* 18: 158–168.

Sarup, Madan. 1996. *Identity, Culture and the Postmodern World.* Edited by Tasneem Raja. Athens, GA: The University of Georgia Press.

Sass, Louis A. 1992. "The Self and Its Vicissitudes in the Psychoanalytic Avant-Garde." In *Constructions of the Self,* ed. George Levine. New Brunswick, NJ: Rutgers University Press, pp. 17–57.

Sassen, Saskia. 1991. *The Global City: New York, London, Tokyo.* Princeton: Princeton University Press.

Sasson-Levy, Orna. 2002. "Constructing Identities at the Margins: Masculinities and Citizenship in the Israeli Army." *The Sociological Quarterly* 43, no. 3: 357–383.

Saxenian, AnnaLee. 1994. *Regional Advantage: Culture and Competition in Silicon Valley and Route 128.* Cambridge, MA: Harvard University Press.

Schonfeld, Erick. 1997. "Have the Urge to Merge? You'd Better Think Twice." *Fortune* 135, no. 6 (March 31): 114–116.

Scott, Susanne G., and Vicki R. Lane. 2000. "Fluid, Fractured, and Distinctive? In Search of a Definition of Organizational Identity." *The Academy of Management Review* 25: 143–144.

Shafir, Gershon, and Yoav Peled. 2002. *Being Israeli: The Dynamics of Multiple Citizenship.* Cambridge: Cambridge University Press.

Sharkansky, Ira. 1996. *Rituals of Conflict: Religion, Politics, and Public Policy in Israel.* Boulder, Colorado: Lynne Rienner Publishers.

Shenhav, Yehouda, and Ely Weitz. 2000. "The Roots of Uncertainty in Organization Theory: A Historical Constructivist Analysis." *Organization* 7(3): 373–401.

Shohat, Ella. 1989. *Israeli Cinema: East/West and the Politics of Representation.* Austin: University of Texas Press.

Sklair, Leslie. 1991. *Sociology of the Global System.* Baltimore, Md.: The Johns Hopkins University Press.

Smooha, Sammi. 1978. *Israel: Pluralism and Conflict.* Berkeley: University of California Press.

Snow, David A., and Leon Anderson. 1987. "Identity Work among the Homeless: The Verbal Construction and Avowal of Personal Identities." *American Journal of Sociology* 92: 1336–1371.

Sobel, Zvi. 1986. *Migrants from the Promised Land.* New Brunswick, NJ: Transaction Books.

Søderberg, Anne-Marie, and Eero Vaara. 2003. *Merging Across Borders: People, Cultures and Politics.* Copenhagen: Copenhagen Business School Press.

Stearns, Linda Brewster, and Kenneth D. Allan. 1996. "Economic Behavior in Institutional Environments: The Corporate Merger Wave of the 1980s." *American Sociological Review* 61 (August): 699–718.

Steensma, H. Kevin, Louis Marino, K. Mark Weaver, and Pat H. Dickson. 2000. "The Influence of National Culture on the Formation of Technology Alliances by Entrepreneurial Firms." *Academy of Management Journal* 43, no. 5: 951–973.

Stone, G.P. 1962. "Appearance and the Self." In *Human Behavior and Social Process: An Interactional Approach*, ed. Arnold M. Rose. London: Routledge & Kegan Paul, pp. 86–119.

Strathern, Marilyn. 1987. "The Limits of Auto-Anthropology." In *Anthropology at Home*, ed. Anthony Jackson. London: Tavistock Publications, pp. 16–37.

Swann, William B. Jr., and Craig A. Hill. 1982. "When Our Identities are Mistaken: Reaffirming Self-Conceptions through Social Interaction." *Journal of Personality and Social Psychology* 43, no. 1: 59–66.

Tayeb, Monir. 1994. "Organizations and National Culture: Methodology Considered." *Organization Studies* 15: 429–446.

Tayeb, Monir. 2001. "Conducting Research across Cultures: Overcoming Drawbacks and Obstacles." *International Journal of Cross Cultural Management* 1: 91–108.

Tedeschi, James T., Svenn Linskold, and Paul Rosenfeld. 1985. *Introduction to Social Psychology*. St. Paul, Minnesota: West Publishing.

Thomas, David C., Elizabeth C. Ravlin, and Alan W. Wallace. 1996. "Effect of Cultural Diversity in Work Groups." *Research in the Sociology of Organizations* 14: 1–33.

Thomas, William Isaac. 1937. *Primitive Behavior.* New York: Mcgraw-Hill.

Thompson, Craig J., and Siok Kuan Tambyah. 1999. "Trying to be a Cosmopolitan." *Journal of Consumer Research* 26 (December): 214–241.

Trice, Harrison Miller. 1993. *Occupational Subcultures in the Workplace.* Ithaca, NY: ILR Press.

Tsui, Anne S., Terri D. Egan, and Charles A. O'Reilly III. 1992. "Being Different: Relational Demography and Organizational Attachment." *Administrative Science Quarterly* 37: 549–579.

Van Maanen, John, and Stephen R. Barley. 1984. "Occupational Communities: Culture and Control in Organizations." *Research in Organizational Behavior* 6: 287–365.

Van Maanen, John. 1979. "The Self, the Situation, and the Rules of Interpersonal Relation." In *Essays in Interpersonal Dynamics,* eds. Waren Bennis, John Van Maanen, Edgar H. Schein, and Fred I. Steele. Homewood, Illinois: The Dorsey Press, pp. 43–101.

Van Maanen, John. 1979b. "Reclaiming Qualitative Methods for Organizational Research: A Preface." In *Qualitative Methodology,* ed. John Van Maanen. Beverly Hills: Sage, pp. 9–18.

Van Maanen, John. 1988. *Tales of the Field: On Writing Ethnography.* Chicago: The University of Chicago Press.

Van Maanen, John. 1992. "Displacing Disney: Some Notes on the Flow of Culture." *Qualitative Sociology* 15, no. 1: 5–35.

Van Maanen, John. 1995. "The End of Innocence: The Ethnography of Ethnography." In *Representation in Ethnography,* ed. John Van Maanen. Thousand Oaks: Sage, pp. 1–35.

Van Maanen, John. 1998. "Studies in Organizational Identity and Change." In *Qualitative Studies of Organizations,* ed. John Van Maanen. Thousand Oaks: Sage, pp. 193–196.

Van Maanen, John. 1998b. "Different Strokes: Qualitative Research in the *Administrative Science Quarterly* from 1956–1996." In *Qualitative Studies of Organizations,* ed. John Van Maanen. Thousand Oaks: Sage, pp. ix-xxxii.

Veiga, John, Michael Lubatkin, Roland Calorie, and Philippe Very. 2000. "Measuring Organizational Culture Clashes: A Two-Nation Post-Hoc Analysis of a Cultural Compatibility Index," *Human Relations* 53, no. 4: 539–557.

Wacquant, Loïc J.D. 1995. "The Pugilistic Point of View: How Boxers Think and Feel about their Trade." *Theory and Society* 24: 489–535.

Weigert, Andrew J. 1983. "Identity: Its Emergence within Sociological Psychology." *Symbolic Interaction* 6, no. 2: 183–206.

Weingrod, Alex (ed.). 1985. *Studies in Israeli Ethnicity: After the Ingathering.* NY: Gordon and Breach Science Publishers.

Weitz, Ely, and Yehouda Shenhav. 2000. "A Longitudinal Analysis of Technical and Organizational Uncertainty in Management Theory. *Organization Studies* 21, no. 1: 243–265.

Whyte, William H. 1956. *The Organization Man.* New York: Simon and Schuster.

Index

Barth, Fredrik, 37, 71, 109, 148n1
Bauman, Zygmunt, 15
Becker, Howard S., 150n1
Beit-Hallahmi, Benjamin, 106
Ben-Ari, Eyal, 9, 61, 71, 96, 112, 138,
    149n5, 149n8, 150n1
Ben-Rafael, Eliezer, 105
Berger, Peter L., 145n15
Bhabha, Homi K., 92, 109, 110
Biggart, Nicole Woolsey, 4
Bilu, Yoram, 149n5
Bliese, Paul D., 146n20
Blumer, Herbert, 10, 144n13
Boyacigiller, Nakiye A., 146n21
Brown, Andrew D., 151n1
Burawoy, Michael, 15, 150n3

Calorie, Roland, 8
Carper, James, 150n1
Castells, Manuel, 2, 3, 143n6
Categorization. See research methods
Child, John, 8, 143n3
Clark, Burton R., 4
Cohen, Anthony P., 60, 82, 108, 130,
    144n8
Cohen, Steven M., 106
Com (pseudonym for parent com-
    pany), 19, 20, 80, 140
    history of, 17–18
    members' references to, 103, 127
    and merger agreement, 18
    See also Globalint (pseudonym for
        merged company); Isrocom
        (pseudonym for company);
        merger (between Isrocom and
        Amerotech)
communication events
    definition of, 29–30, 37
    face-to-face, 37, 50–64, 73, 134
    and local-organizational identity
        construction, 48–50, 58–64, 73,
        82, 84–85, 134–135
    managerial participation in, 38,
        41–44, 51–59, 60–61
    technologically mediated, 37,
        38–50, 58–64, 134

See also communication processes;
    cross-cultural interactions;
    email; exclusion; local-organiza-
    tional identity; meeting; social
    construction; training events
communication processes
    merger integration of, 29–30; 33–34,
    134
    See also communication events;
        information technology (IT)
communications technology. See email;
    information technology (IT);
    intranet
company culture. See organizational
    culture
computer programmers
    comparisons of, 114–116, 121,
        129–130
    role, 25–26, 151n5
    self-criticism of, 116
    See also occupational identities;
        R&D (Research and Develop-
        ment) Department
conference call meeting, 38–44, 48–50,
    60–63
    See also communication events;
        communication processes;
        information technology (IT);
        meeting; social construction,
        global technology as instru-
        ment of
Cooley, Charles Horton, 5
Corley, Kevin G., 151n1
corporate culture. See organizational
    culture
cosmopolitan identity, 9
co-subordination identity
    conceptualization of, 111, 150n2,
        150n3
    as global bonds, 123–124, 126–131,
        136, 137, 138
    in the mold of the "us"/"them"
        split, 98, 112, 121–123,
        129–130, 136
    See also identity; identity dilem-
        mas; Israeli identity and work

history of, 91–92, 149nn10–11,
    149n2
and Jewish identity, 91, 105–106,
    149nn10–11
and the military, 96–97
See also Americanization; Hebrew;
    hierarchy, global; high-tech
    sector, Israeli; Israeli identity;
    Jewish identity; military, Is-
    raeli; national culture; national
    identity; nationalism, Israeli
Isrocom (pseudonym for company)
    ethnographic study of, 10–15
    founding of, 17
    globalization of, 17–34, 133–134
    history of, 17–19, 22, 24, 33
    merger celebration at, 1–2, 3, 9, 133,
        140
    merger transformation of, 19–34,
        133–134, 147n4, 147n8
    organizational culture of, 30–31, 34
    organizational politics in, 22–24
    pre-merger Israeliness of, 17–19, 33,
        133–134
    top management of, 21–23, 33
    underlying work process in, 24, 27
    See also Com (pseudonym for parent
        company); ethnography; Glo-
        balint (pseudonym for merged
        company); global organiza-
        tions; high-tech organizations;
        Israeli identity; Israeli society;
        local-organizational identity;
        merger (between Isrocom and
        Amerotech); Net (pseudonym
        for Isrocom's product); organi-
        zational globalization; organiza-
        tional identity

Jack, Gavin, 109
Jackall, Robert, 151n3
Jackson, Anthony, 146n22
Jackson, Brad, 148n3
Jacobson, Carol K., 146n20
Jenkins, Richard, 144n9
Jermier, John M., 4

Jewish identity, 69, 79, 148n3, 149n6
and the Israeli/American dichoto-
    my, 106–107, 108
and Israeli identity, 91, 105–107,
    148n2, 149n2, 149n10
and the secular/religious distinc-
    tion, 75–76, 82, 89, 90,91, 93,
    105, 106, 148n2, 149n11
See also identity; Israeli identity;
    Israeli society; local-organi-
    zational identity and Jewish
    identity; multiple identities;
    nationalism, Israeli
joint ventures, 2, 146n20
See also mergers and acquisitions;
    organizational globalization

Kanungo, Rabindra N., 146n20
Karmark, Esben, 149n12
Katriel, Tamar, 91
Khazzoom, Aziza, 92, 149n2
Kilduff, Martin, 144n11
Kimmerling, Baruch, 91, 92, 96, 106,
    149n2, 149n10
King, Anthony D., 65
Klapp, Orrin Edgar, 143n8
Knights, David, 4
Kondo, Dorrine K., 4, 6, 7, 145n18,
    150n3
Kovacs, George L., 146n20
Kramer, Roderick M., 4, 144n10
Kunda, Gideon, 4, 61, 138, 148n3,
    150n1, 150n3
Kunda, Ziva, 144n9, 149n1

Laclau, Ernesto, 49
Lane, Vicki R., 151n1
language
    merger standardization of, 30, 33
    methodological issues pertaining to,
        14, 146n23
    as symbolic resource, 48, 61
    See also exclusion, linguistic; He-
        brew
Lavie, Smadar, 6
Levine, George, 145n16

of the researcher, 13–15
technological monitoring of, 49–50, 63
See also American identity; communication events; co-subordination identity; gender identities; global-organizational identity; Goffman, Erving; identity; immigrant identity; Interactionists; Israeli identity; local-organizational identity; national identity; occupational identities; organizational identity; postmodernism; representations; self; social construction

narratives
in ethnographic writing, 13
of identity dilemmas, 124–131, 137, 138, 139
of merger history, 119
national identities as, 92
organizational identities as, 6
national culture
management treatment of, 30–34
See also American identity; crosscultural interactions; crosscultural research; Israeli identity; Israeli society; mergers and acquisitions (M&As) and national culture clash; national identity
national generalizations. *See* American identity; Israeli identity; national identity, social construction of; stereotypes
national identity
and the construction of local-organization identity, 2, 9, 61, 63, 76–77, 83, 84, 90, 93–110, 134, 135–139
cross-cultural perspective on, 8–9, 61, 84, 108–109, 145nn19–20
as cultural hybrid, 91–92
as discursive device, 92

essentialist concept of, 8–10, 61–62, 84, 108–109, 137–138
in global organizations, 7–10, 61–62, 84, 131, 137–138, 145nn19–20
as imagined community, 92, 110
as narration, 92
as personality template, 93–103, 106–110, 113, 116, 120, 121, 135, 136
as political resource, 23
social construction of, 9–10, 61, 84, 93–110, 135–139
as stereotype, 9, 93–103, 108, 110, 113, 116, 120, 124, 135, 136, 138
as symbolic resource, 2, 61–62, 63, 84, 97, 101, 108, 110, 124, 138, 148n3
and work identities, 113–114, 115, 116, 120, 122, 123–124, 130, 136
See also American identity; Anderson, Benedict; identity; Israeli society; Israeli identity; local-organizational identity; national culture
nationalism, Israeli, 105, 149n2, 149n10
See also Israeli identity; Israeli society; military, Israeli; national identity
nationality. *See* national identity
Net (pseudonym for Isrocom's product)
compared to Amerotech's product, 115–116
intranet representation of, 80
See also computer programmers; Isrocom (pseudonym for company); R&D (Research and Development) Department; technology
Nord, Walter R., 4
normative control, 150n3
See also Kunda, Gideon

occupational identities
conceptualization of, 111–112; 150n1

organizational politics
  and communication events, 42,
    44–48, 63
  post-merger, 22–23, 24, 33, 128
  pre-merger, 22
  See also authority; formal power;
    hierarchy; representations and
    organizational power; repre-
    sentations, strategic
organizational structure
  contesting, 24, 45
  and corporate globalization, 2–3,
    143n6
  of Globalint, 21–29, 33, 147nn3–4,
    147n8
  merger transformations of, 21–29,
    33, 134, 147n4, 147n8
  See also authority; Customer Sup-
    port Department; Finance
    Department; formal power;
    hierarchy; Human Resources
    (HR) Department; Marketing
    Departments; Operations De-
    partment; R&D (Research and
    Development) Department
Ó Riain, Seán, 4, 143n6

participant observation. *See* research
  methods
Peled, Yoav, 91
personal identity, 79, 144n9, 144n14,
  145n15
Peterson, Mark F., 146n20
Peterson, Richard B., 146n20
Pitkethly, Robert, 8, 143n3
politics, organizational. *See* organizational politics
postcolonialism, 110
postmodernism
  and concept of identity, 5–6, 139
  and concept of self, 6, 62–63, 90,
    139, 145nn16–17, 148n4
  and ethnographic writing, 13
  and globalization, 6
  See also self, decentered
post-structuralism, 145n16

See also Derrida, Jacques; postmodernism
power. *See* authority; formal power;
  hierarchy; organizational politics
Pratt, Michael G., 4
professional identities. *See* occupational identities
project managers (marketing
  engineers)
  comparisons of, 112–114, 121
  role, 25, 147n6, 151n5
  self-criticism of, 114
  See also Marketing Departments;
    occupational identities
Pugh, Derek S., 146n20

R&D (Research and Development)
  Department
  categories of employees in, 25–26,
    147n7
  a review meeting in, 67–69
  structural merger integration of,
    25–27
  top management of, 21
  work in, 26
  and the work process, 24, 27
  See also computer programmers;
    Customer Support Depart-
    ment; Finance Department;
    Globalint (pseudonym for
    merged company); Human
    Resources (HR) Department;
    Isrocom (pseudonym for
    company); Marketing Depart-
    ments; merger integration
    teams; Net (pseudonym for
    Isrocom's product); Opera-
    tions Department; organiza-
    tional structure; technology
racial identity, 144n13, 145n19
Radford, Mark H. B., 146n20
Rafaeli, Anat, 4
Ram, Uri, 92
Rao, Hayagreeva, 144n10
Ravlin, Elizabeth C., 146no20
Raz-Krakotzkin, Amnon, 91